Accounting for Costs as Fixed and Variable

By

Maryanne M. Mowen, Ph.D., CMA
School of Accounting
College of Business Administration
Oklahoma State University

A study carried out on behalf of the
National Association of Accountants
Montvale, New Jersey

Published by

National Association of Accountants
10 Paragon Drive, Montvale, NJ 07645-1760
Donna Marks, Editor
Mandel & Wagreich, Inc., Cover

NAA Publication Number 85180
ISBN 0-86641-117-8

Foreword

Now that management accounting has been practiced as a profes-
sion for some time, many of the traditional methods and techniques
have acquired a still more purposeful meaning. As management accountants think of their jobs in a new way, they need techniques,
new and old, which will enable them to act differently — at a higher
level of responsibility for corporate decisions. It is important to
recognize as well that now some of the traditional accounting dilem-
mas have a more direct and prominent bearing on the effectiveness
of executive decision making. These were the principle reasons for
the preparation of this report.

Presented here are the results of a study of fixed and variable costs.
The report is from the perspective of a manager who must understand the meaning of the fixed-variable cost distinction and who must
be able to take this into account within a specific decision-making
context. It must be clear also that changing organizational settings
and business conditions require a careful choice of the method to be
applied in the process of identifying the costs as fixed or variable
for various types of business decisions and reports. In many in-
stances, it will be desirable, perhaps mandatory, that this identification be considered a part of the overall decision process. In principle
at least, all who have a share in the decisions or in the responsibility
of carrying out the decisions should understand the fixed/variable
cost identification process.

Guidance in the course of the research work and in the preparation of this report was generously and kindly provided by the Project Committee:

Robert E. Hampel
Keller-Crescent Co.
Evansville, Ind.

James L. Crandall
Monroe Egg Farm, Inc.
Plainfield, Ill.

Margaret Duffy
Arthur Andersen & Co.
New York, N.Y.

The report reflects the views of the researcher and not necessarily those of the Association, the Committee on Research, or the Project Committee.

Appreciation is extended to Stephen Landekich, former director of research, for his guidance and assistance.

Patrick Romano
Director of Research
National Association of Accountants

Acknowledgments

Many people assisted me in compiling the information I needed to write this book. I am grateful to each one of them and would like to formally acknowledge them here.

The following individuals gave invaluable assistance in completing the survey:

Price Brattin	Price Waterhouse & Co.
R. E. Crips	Conoco Chemicals
Larry Cuff	General Motors Assembly Plant
Rocky Duckworth	Peat, Marwick, Mitchell & Co.
Hal W. Ellis	Stillwater Flight Center, Inc.
Roger A. Hanes	Unarco Rubber Products
Randy Harbour	Phillips Petroleum Co.
William S. Houston	Houston and Co.
Roseann K. Kubicek	Phillips Petroleum Co.
Dale May	Celestial Seasonings
Richard W. Mendick	*The Denver Post*
Stephen J. Miller	Great Expectations
Dorman Morsman	Kimray, Inc.
John A. Riggs	Stillwater Medical Center
Paul Smith	ARO, Inc.
Mimi Sherlock	Sylvester Industries
Sandra Lee Swearingen	Certified Public Accountant
Larry Watkins	Certified Public Accountant
Donald L. Young	OGE Co.

In addition, people from the following companies were very helpful: Champlin Petroleum, Inc.; Union Pacific Corp.; Frontier Engineering, Inc.; and CMI Corp. Finally, there were several participants in the survey who preferred to remain anonymous. Their contribution also is appreciated.

The writing of this book benefited greatly from the contributions of several people. Stephen Landekich provided invaluable suggestions in editing the material. Members of the NAA Research Subcommittee, Robert E. Hampel, James L. Crandall, and Margaret Duffy, generously donated their time to review earlier versions of this book. Finally, I appreciate the research assistance of David Auer and Janet Hacker and the skillful word processing help of Pam Laufer and Laura Davis.

Maryanne M. Mowen, Ph.D., CMA

About the Author

Maryanne M. Mowen, CMA, is associate professor of accounting in the School of Accounting, Oklahoma State University, Stillwater, Oklahoma. In her seven years at OSU, she has taught a variety of courses including financial and managerial principles, cost accounting, management accounting for MBAs, and graduate management accounting. The courses have spanned the sophomore through master's level.

Prof. Mowen earned a B.A. in history from The Colorado College and M.S. and Ph.D. degrees in economics from Arizona State University. She completed postgraduate work in accounting at Oklahoma State University. Prof. Mowen passed the CMA examination in 1981 with a Certificate of Distinguished Performance.

Currently her research interests focus on management decision making, especially on how the use of heuristics and framing either help or hinder the decision process. In addition to this book for the National Association of Accountants, she has published articles in a variety of accounting and business publications.

Table of Contents

Chapter 6

Chapter 7

Chapter 1

Introduction

This book is designed to be a reference guide for the management accountant who needs information about the separation and uses of fixed and variable costs. Topics covered include: the conceptual background of fixed and variable costs, methods of separating total cost into fixed and variable components, a review of the accounting literature in this area, a survey of firms which use fixed and variable costs in decision making, and three case studies. The survey consisted of telephone and personal interviews with financial executives of 25 companies regarding their experiences with fixed and variable cost separation and use. By far the most popular method of cost separation was managerial judgment. The survey showed that fixed and variable costs were used for a wide variety of purposes; those most frequently cited included pricing, profitability analysis, and breakeven analysis.

Management accountants know that it is important to recognize the impact of volume changes on related costs. *Separating and Using Costs as Fixed and Variable,* Accounting Practice Report 10, published by the National Association of Accountants in June 1960, cites experiences such as the following:

> The distinction between variable and fixed overhead is extremely useful in control and in formulating managerial policies. Responsibility for excess fixed costs usually rests with general or major production executives, whereas the responsibility for changes in variable costs falls upon minor production executives. (page 28)
>
> Because we segregate all fixed and variable costs, we gain the advantage of being able to advise management quickly and easily the dollars of sales required to break even and the unit volume needed plus other key figures, per year, month, week or day! . . . Any accountant who has been asked to supply similar figures and has not segregated fixed and variable expense in his cost system can verify the headache involved in trying to develop these data after the fact. (page 32)

In the 25 years since the publication of Accounting Practice Report 10, knowledge of fixed and variable cost separation has continued to be regarded as an important analytical tool. During that time, the use of fixed and variable costs has become more widespread, although the state-of-the-art in separation methods has not changed radically. Factors leading to this increased interest include the impact of economic expansion and recession on cost patterns, the increased importance of service industries, the advent of greater mechanization in basic industries, and the introduction of robotics. In addition, cost separation is easier now because of the widespread availability of computers and improved databases. As a result, management has been more likely to support efforts to develop information on the separation and use of fixed and variable costs.

This book represents an advance in three areas. First, relevant accounting literature on fixed and variable costs is reviewed; this literature was virtually nonexistent 10 years ago. Second, the statistical methods used to separate fixed and variable costs have been refined, and these refinements are discussed here. Third, the survey of firms undertaken for this study reflects the economic and technological changes that have occurred. Firms from a variety of industries and a range of size were surveyed to give a feel for the diversity of uses to which fixed and variable cost analysis can be put. In summary, the objective of this book is to describe the separation and uses of fixed and variable cost analysis advocated by both theorists and managers.

This book is organized into the following sections: conceptual background, methods of separating fixed and variable costs, review of the literature, survey methodology and results, and three case studies. The conceptual background reviews concepts necessary to the analysis of fixed and variable costs. For example, terminology and assumptions, such as the concepts of the time horizon and relevant range, are discussed. These concepts form the basis for the presentation of cost separation methods: the high-low method; the scattergraph method; the method of ordinary least squares; and managerial judgment. The sample calculations for each method are based on a single set of cost data so that differences among the methods are more readily apparent. Advantages and disadvantages of each method also are discussed.

The literature review is divided into four subsections for the convenience of the reader. These subsections are: some concerns about fixed and variable cost usage; the impact of high tech on fixed and variable cost patterns; examples of fixed and variable cost usage;

and two assessments of fixed and variable cost separation by manufacturing firms.

The next section of the book presents results of the survey of companies' experience with fixed and variable cost usage. The sample selection and survey methodology are described. Then results are presented.

Three case studies are presented to demonstrate the use of fixed and variable costs by companies. The first presents the standard direct costing system for a petroleum refinery. The second discusses breakeven analysis for a greeting card manufacturer. The third concerns budgeting in a not-for-profit hospital.

Finally, an annotated bibliography is provided at the end of the book for those wishing more information. Articles and books are categorized according to their primary themes: characteristics of fixed and variable costs, methods of cost separation, and/or applications to decision making.

Chapter 2

Conceptual Background

In order for a manager to analyze the firm's cost structure properly, he or she must know how costs respond to changes in volume.
All costs do not react in the same way. One cost might move in one
direction as the result of a particular action, while another might
not change. Unless the behavior pattern of each cost is understood
clearly, the impact of a firm's activity on its costs will not be known
until after the activity has occurred. Clearly, then, knowledge of cost
behavior has important implications for planning.

Cost behavior is the general term for determining whether a cost
is fixed or variable in relation to changes in volume or activity. A
cost that remains the same in total as activity increases or decreases
is a fixed cost. A variable cost is one that increases with an increase
in activity and decreases with a decrease in activity. Determining
whether a cost is fixed or variable depends crucially on the time
horizon. In the short run, a cost cannot be changed and, therefore,
is fixed. In the long run, all costs are variable, Paradoxically, it is
the fixed or variable nature of the costs that defines the short or long
run, not a predetermined time length that defines the fixity of costs.
Therefore, managers must consider a number of factors when determining cost behavior, ranging from statistical techniques, to definitions, to management philosophy.

Theoretically, separating fixed and variable costs is no problem.
In fact, most economics textbooks simply assume that the cost
separation has been accomplished and proceed from there. It is the
management accountant who must bring cost separation from theory
to reality. Before cost separation methods can be described, it is
necessary to start with the definitions of some important terms: the
short run, cost formula, relevant range, and activity level. The short
run is the period of time during which a cost is fixed. The cost formula describes the way the cost-volume relationship is reduced to

algebraic form. Knowledge of the cost formula makes it easier to forecast costs. The relevant range refers to the range of volume over which the cost-volume relationship described by the cost formula is stable. Activity level can be measured in a number of ways, such as direct labor hours or units produced. These four concepts are discussed further below.

The Short Run

One problem in distinguishing between fixed and variable costs is the length of the short run. Different costs have different-length short runs. The length of the short-run period depends to some extent on management judgment. Within the short-run period, costs are treated as fixed. Fixed costs may be described as programmable, discretionary, or committed. Programmable fixed costs are easy to change, sometimes within one week. For example, maintenance labor may be increased or decreased rapidly by hiring or firing workers. Discretionary fixed costs are those subject to annual review. They could be changed relatively quickly but typically are not. The advertising expense budget usually is a discretionary fixed cost. Committed fixed costs represent long-term investments in property, plant, and equipment. These costs usually are the most difficult to change.

The Cost Formula

Cost behavior can be described most conveniently by using a formula. Typically, cost is assumed to be a straight-line function of activity level with all other factors held constant. Thus, cost is expressed as

$$C = a + bQ$$

where
C = total cost
Q = activity level (for example, quantity produced or sold)
a = the fixed component of total cost
b = the variable rate

For a strictly fixed cost (see Figure 1), a is some amount and b is zero, meaning the cost is the same (for example, $1,000) no matter what the activity level. For a strictly variable cost (see Figure 2), a is zero and b is some per-unit cost (for example, $1.50). Then, as Quantity increases so does cost. If a and b are greater than

Figure 1
STRICTLY FIXED COST

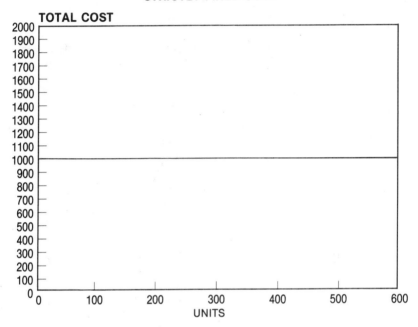

Figure 2
STRICTLY VARIABLE COST

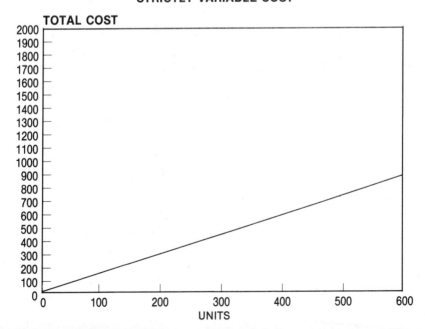

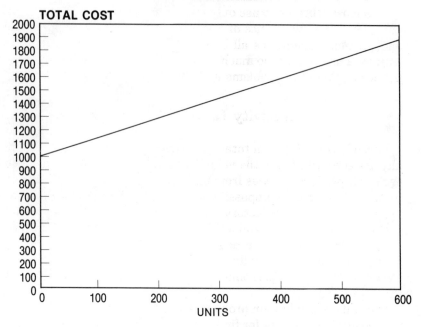

Figure 3
SEMIVARIABLE COST

zero, the cost is semivariable or mixed (see Figure 3). Thus, if $C = 1,000 + 1.50*Q$, then total cost would be $1,000 at zero units of activity, and it would be $1,150 at an activity level of 100.

Of course, cost does not have to bear a linear relationship with activity level. That is just the simplest relationship and by far the easiest one to estimate. Many other relationships are possible.

The Relevant Range

The relevent range is the range of volumes over which the firm can reasonably expect total fixed cost, per-unit variable cost, and selling price to be constant. Firms usually will have several relevent ranges leading to several cost-volume relationships. As a result, a different $C = a + bQ$ equation must be developed for the various levels of volume. The concept of relevant range is designed to narrow the planner's frame of reference to include only the potential activity levels and to exclude those which are obviously inappropriate.

Thus, the relevant range is a tool which makes the separation of fixed and variable cost easier in practice.

It is most efficient to use only one cost equation for each type of cost. Therefore, the choice of relevant range is important. A small enough range eliminates all but one cost formula, but it may introduce a problem of too much restriction of the range for planning purposes. Potential problems and solutions are discussed later.

Activity Level Measures

Variable costs move in total with changes in activity level. Usually the activity level is the volume of production. Tracing costs to each unit produced ranges from relatively easy (for example, direct materials) to virtually impossible (for example, janitorial services or property taxes on the factory building). For service firms, tracing costs to their units of production may be even more troublesome. Is the appropriate unit an hour of service or the performance of a particular task? Additionally, some units of service may be provided by more experienced personnel, leading to "deluxe" service versus the "standard" model.

The units of production problem often is sidestepped by considering the original purpose for finding an appropriate activity measure — which is to predict the level of total cost by breaking it down into its fixed and variable components. For example, electrical cost may be a function of machine hours, shipping expense may be a function of units sold, and hospital laundry cost may be a function of patient days. The choice of activity measure is tailored not only to the particular firm, but also to the particular cost being measured. Statistical techniques, such as correlation analysis, described in Chapter 3 can assist the management accountant in selecting the most appropriate activity measure for each type of cost being analyzed.

Chapter 3

Methods of Separating Fixed and Variable Costs

The separation of fixed and variable costs can be accomplished by four methods which run the gamut from statistical to judgment based. The choice of method depends on a variety of factors. Each method separates the fixed from the variable components and depends on the use of historical data, or past observations, such as those given in Table 1. Each has inherent advantages and disadvantages which make it appropriate in some situations but not in others. For example, managerial judgment is considered to be quicker, simpler, and less expensive than a statistical method. However, if the decision being made is highly sensitive to errors in classifying costs as fixed or variable, a more precise method (such as ordinary least squares) will give better results. Unfortunately, no one method is clearly superior.

Before cost separation methods are discussed, a numerical example is presented in Table 1. It consists of 12 monthly observations of utilities expense (the dependent variable) and units produced (the independent variable, x). This example will be used to illustrate each cost separation method. Additional calculations which will be needed later also are given in Table 1.

There are four cost separation methods: the high-low method, the scattergraph method, the method of ordinary least squares, and managerial judgment. The computational technique and advantages and disadvantages for each are discussed.

The High-Low Method

The high-low method consists of taking two cost-volume data points to estimate a line. The slope of the line is the variable rate,

Table 1

Month	Units	Utilities Cost	(x-x)	(y-y)	(x-x) (y-y)	(x-x)²	(y-y)²
Jan.	900	$ 4,000	50	250	12,500	2,500	62,500
Feb.	650	3,300	− 200	− 450	90,000	40,000	202,500
Mar.	500	2,500	− 350	− 1,250	437,500	122,500	1,562,500
Apr.	800	3,500	− 50	− 250	12,500	2,500	62,500
May	1,000	4,500	150	750	112,500	22,500	562,500
June	1,200	4,600	350	850	297,500	122,500	722,000
July	750	3,600	− 100	− 150	15,000	10,000	22,500
Aug.	600	3,000	− 250	− 750	187,500	62,500	562,500
Sept.	850	3,750	0	0	0	0	0
Oct.	700	3,250	− 150	− 500	75,000	22,500	250,000
Nov.	950	4,000	100	250	25,000	10,000	62,500
Dec.	1,300	5,000	450	1,250	562,500	202,500	1,562,500
TOTAL	10,200	$45,000	0	0	1,827,500	620,000	5,635,000

AVERAGES: $\bar{x}$ = 850 $\bar{y}$ = $ 3,750

and the y-intercept is the fixed cost. Figure 4 shows the cost-volume pairs given in Table 1 plotted on a graph. Maintenance cost per month is shown on the y-axis, and production volume is shown on the x-axis. December is the month with the highest maintenance expense and March is the month with the lowest. The line drawn through these two points describes the high-low relationship. While the variable rate and fixed cost component of maintenance expense could be read directly off the graph, it is much simpler and clearer to solve for these two cost components using the following equations:

$$\text{Variable Rate} = \frac{\text{Highest month's expense - Lowest month's expense}}{\text{Highest month's volume - Lowest month's volume}}$$

Fixed Cost   = Total expense - [(variable rate) (month's volume)]

For the data from Table 1,

Variable Rate = (5,000 − 2,500)/(1,300 − 500) = $3.125

Fixed Cost   = 5,000 − 3.125(1,300) = 2,500 − 3.125(500) = $937.50

Note that the fixed cost component can be figured using either the high cost-volume data point or the low cost-volume data point.

Figure 4
HIGH-LOW METHOD

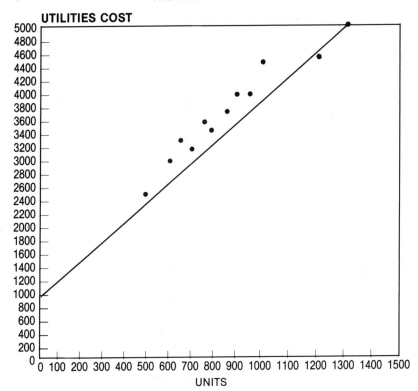

Advantages of the high-low method are: It is easy to compute, it is easy to understand, and it is objective. Disadvantages are: It uses only two data points, and if either data point is extreme, the results will be skewed; and only the impact of one independent variable is permitted. The method of least squares can take care of both disadvantages.

The Scattergraph Method

The scattergraph or scatterplot method of determining fixed and variable cost components consists of plotting cost data on a graph. As in the previous examples, cost is measured on the vertical axis, and the independent variable is measured on the horizontal axis. All data points are plotted on the graph, and a straight line is drawn as close to as many of the points as possible (that is, a straight line is fitted to the points by inspection). Usually as many data points lie above the line as below it. A line fitted by inspection to the data from Table 1 is shown in Figure 5.

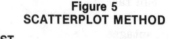

Figure 5
SCATTERPLOT METHOD

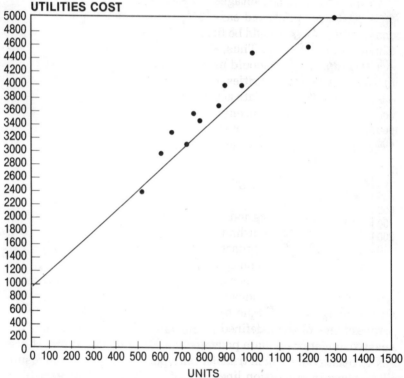

The line just drawn is a regression line. On average, the intercept, the point at which the regression line intersects the cost axis, represents total fixed cost. The slope of the regression line represents the average variable cost. These representations can be figured in the following way. Fixed cost simply is read off the y-axis; using the numerical example and Figure 5, it is $950. Variable cost is average variable cost divided by average number of units produced, or $(3,750 - 950)/850 = \$3.294$.

The scattergraph method has some disadvantages. First, it is subjective; any two people given the same data will draw different lines and, hence, have different estimates of fixed and variable costs. As a result, the line shown in Figure 5 is not the unique "correct" line; it is the author's best estimate. The reader's estimate would no doubt be different yet equally "correct." Second, the variable rate must be computed from the slope, and the fixed rate must be read from the y-intercept, a difficult task if the scale of the graph is not large enough.

Despite these disadvantages, the scattergraph offers advantages. It is relatively quick and easy. More important, while it suggests that a straight line should be fitted to the data, clearly nonlinear relationships are revealed. Thus, some analysts have suggested that a scattergraph always should be done first in conjunction with other methods. Any nonlinearities or discontinuities in the data then can be spotted and appropriate action taken (for example, redefining the relevant range to include only the linear portion, or estimating two or more cost/volume relationships, or specifying a nonlinear relationship when using ordinary least squares).

The Method of Ordinary Least Squares

The most precise method of determining the fixed and variable components of cost is ordinary least squares (OLS), or regression. This is a statistical approach to the scattergraph method.

Basically, the regression approach is to fit the best line to the data points — the one which is closest to as many of the points as possible. That is the same idea as the scattergraph method. However, OLS refines the technique by providing an algorithm which finds the best line. Best is defined as the one for which the sum of the squared deviations of data points from the regression line is smallest.

The calculations which transform a set of observations on cost and volume into a regression line $(Y = a + bX)$ are as follows:

Variable Rate: $b = \Sigma (x - \overline{x})(y - \overline{y})/\Sigma (x - \overline{x})^2 = 1{,}827{,}500/620{,}000 = \$2.95/\text{unit}$

Fixed Cost: $Y = a + bX$

$$3{,}750 = a + 2.95(850)$$

$$a = \$1{,}242.50$$

Hence, the formula for the regression line in this case is
Y = $1,242.50 + $2.95X. Any level of output in the relevant range
can be entered as X to predict utilities cost Y.

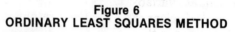

Figure 6
ORDINARY LEAST SQUARES METHOD

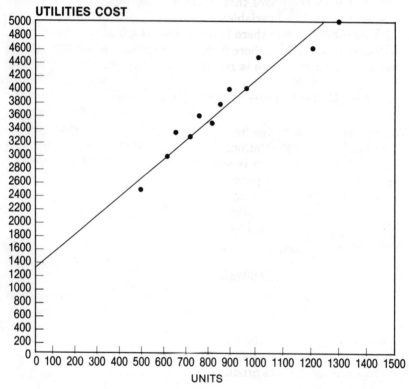

In Figure 6, the actual cost/volume data points for the numerical
example and the regression line calculated with OLS are plotted. Using May's cost and volume as an example, the predicted total cost
of 1,000 units of output can be read off the regression line. It is
$1,242.50 + 2.95(1,000) = $4,192.50. Actual cost for May was $4,500.
The $307.50 difference between predicted and actual cost is the devia-
tion. These deviations are computed for every data point, squared
and summed. The regression line is the line for which the sum of these
squared deviations is smallest. This is the sense in which OLS com-
putes the best regression line.

It is clear that OLS finds the best regression line for X and Y. Additional computations may be done to see how good a job X does in predicting Y. Is X a good predictor variable or might another independent variable do a better job? In simple regression, where there is only one independent variable, the coefficient of correlation, r, can be computed. The coefficient of correlation does not show causality. That is, it does not prove that X causes Y or vice versa. Instead, it shows how well two variables move together. When X rises (falls) and Y also rises (falls), there is positive correlation. When X rises (falls) and Y falls (rises), there is negative correlation. Finally, when there is no pattern, there is no correlation.

$$r = [\Sigma (x - \bar{x})(y - \bar{y})] / \sqrt{[\Sigma (x - \bar{x})^2 \Sigma (y - \bar{y})^2]}$$

The values for r can range from -1 (perfect negative correlation) to 1 (perfect positive correlation). Values close to zero denote no correlation. If r is squared, it is shown as R^2 and denotes the percentage of variation in the dependent variable which is explained by the independent variable. The coefficient of determination, R^2, ranges from 0 (no variation is explained) to 1 (all variations in the dependent variable are explained by the independent variable). Using the above data,

$$r = 1,827,500/(620,000)(563,500) = .98$$

$$R^2 = .96$$

Clearly, with r of .98, the number of units produced and utilities expense are very highly positively correlated. R^2 equal to .96 shows that the number of units produced explains nearly all the variations in utilities expense.

Analyzing coefficients of correlation and determination is one means of determining how good the regression equation is. Another statistic which helps to see how good the regression results are for predicting values of the dependent variable is the standard error of the estimate. Of course, it would be highly unlikely that the regression equation would be able to predict cost exactly. The question then becomes how much deviation of actual from predicted should be expected — or tolerated.

The standard error of the estimate is the standard deviation about the regression line. It can be used to construct a confidence interval. Using normal curve probabilities, approximately 68% of the data points are expected to lie within one standard error of the regression line; about 95% lie within two standard errors; and about 99% within three standard errors.

The standard error of the estimate is

$$ SE = \sqrt{\Sigma\,(y - y_e)^2/(n - 2)} $$

where y = actual value

y_e = y value predicted by regression equation

Table 2 shows computations needed to figure the standard error of the estimate.

Table 2

Month	Units	Utilities Cost	Predicted Cost	Difference	Difference Squared
Jan.	900	$ 4,000	$ 3,897.50	102.50	10,506.25
Feb.	650	3,300	3,160.00	140.00	19,600.00
Mar.	500	2,500	2,717.50	− 217.50	47,306.25
Apr.	800	3,500	3,602.50	− 102.50	10,506.25
May	1,000	4,500	4,192.50	370.50	94,556.25
June	1,200	4,600	4,782.50	− 182.50	33,306.25
July	750	3,600	3,455.00	145.00	21,025.00
Aug.	600	3,000	3,012.50	− 12.50	156.25
Sept.	850	3,750	3,750.00	0	0
Oct.	700	3,250	3,307.50	− 57.50	3,306.25
Nov.	950	4,000	4,045.00	− 45.00	2,025.00
Dec.	1,300	5,000	5,077.50	− 77.50	6,006.25
TOTAL	10,200	$45,000	$45,000.00	0	248,300.00

$$ SE = (248{,}300)/(12 - 2) = 24{,}830 = 157.58 $$

Suppose the firm wanted to check the July utility expense. At $3,600 actual versus $3,455 predicted for the 750 units produced, it has a deviation of $145, which is within one standard error of the predicted value. Thus, this deviation does not appear to be "large" given the information on hand. More data points or smaller average deviations would result in a smaller standard error and a narrower confidence interval.

OLS has several advantages. It uses more data points than the high-low method and is therefore less subject to the influence of outliers. OLS is more precise than the scattergraph method; different individuals using OLS on a set of data will compute the same fixed component and variable rate. OLS can provide additional information about the cost relationship through related statistics (for example, the coefficients of correlation and determination, and the standard error of the estimate). If multiple regression is used, the impact of more than one independent variable on the dependent variable can be examined. Finally, OLS can be used to estimate certain nonlinear relationships (for example, by converting the values of the variables in logarithms).

Managerial Judgment

Managerial judgment is by far the most widely used method in practice. Many managers simply use their experience and past observation of cost-volume relationships to determine fixed and variable costs. Even this method, however, may take a number of forms. Some managers simply assign particular costs to the fixed category and others to the variable category. They ignore the possibility of semivariable costs. Thus, a chemical firm may regard materials and utilities as strictly variable and all other costs as fixed. Even labor, the textbook example of a variable cost, may be fixed for this firm. The appeal of this method is simplicity. Before opting for this course, management would do well to make sure that each cost is predominantly fixed or variable and that the decisions being made are not highly sensitive to errors in computing the nature of costs as fixed or variable.

Management may instead divide individual costs into fixed and variable components by deciding just what the fixed and variable parts are — that is, using experience to say that a certain amount of a cost is fixed and that, therefore, the rest must be variable. Then the variable component can be computed using one or more cost/volume data points. This has the advantage of accounting for semivariable costs but is subject to a similar type of error as the strict fixed/variable dichotomy. That is, management may be wrong in its assessment.

Finally, management may use experience and judgment to refine statistical estimation results. Perhaps the experienced manager might "eyeball" the data and throw out several points as being highly unusual, or the manager might revise results of estimation to take account of projected changes in cost structure or technology.

Statistical techniques are highly accurate in depicting the past —
but they cannot foresee the future, which is, of course, what management really wants.

The advantage of using managerial judgment to separate fixed and
variable costs is its simplicity. In situations where the manager has
a deep understanding of the firm and its cost patterns, this method
can give good results. However, if the manager does not have good
judgment, errors will occur. Therefore, it is important to consider
the experience of the manager, the potential for error, and the effect
that error could have on related decisions.

Chapter 4

Review of the Literature

The review of the literature seeks to provide a linkage between the theoretical approach of methods of cost separation and the experiential approach of the survey. As such, this section reviews the literature on fixed and variable costs from a practical viewpoint by addressing "real" problems and offering workable solutions. The literature which will be reviewed has been aimed at management accountants rather than academicians. Therefore, it is more current than information found in textbooks, but it is not necessarily at the cutting edge of accounting change. It is the goal of the survey in Chapter 5 to give the most recent information on current managerial practices involving fixed and variable costing.

This literature review is organized as follows. First, the background and some concerns regarding fixed and variable cost usage are discussed. Second, the impact of high technology is detailed. The third section presents examples of situations in which firms relied heavily on fixed and variable cost separation. Finally, the results of surveys by the NAA and other researchers are compared.

Some Concerns About Fixed and Variable Cost Usage

Usage of fixed and variable cost classifications increased as management accounting began to come into its own in the early 1950s. Analysis of cost behavior was considered crucial in the decision making called for in a period of industrial expansion. Fixed costs were generally dismissed as sunk, and variable costs were considered both controllable and relevant in pricing, productivity analysis, and performance evaluation decisions. While that treatment of fixed and variable costs may have been appropriate then, some changes have occurred recently in the economic environment which make fixed and variable cost classification more difficult (Whiting, 1981). These changes include: a shift toward capital intensive production, a trend toward viewing labor as a fixed factor of production, the growing importance of product as opposed to divisional profitability analysis, the growing proportion of total costs represented by semivariable energy costs, the proliferation of service industries, and the recent experience with business contraction rather than expansion. These environmental changes led Whiting to make the following observations regarding fixed and variable cost usage.

Observation 1

The impact of the time horizon on decisions is often overlooked. Because all costs are variable in the long run, fixed costs can exist only in the short run. Then one must ask: is the cost short run or long run; what is the length of the short run period; does the length of the short run differ among cost categories? The shorter the time period under consideration, the relatively more fixed cost tends to be. A firm which relies on a formally published classification of costs into fixed and variable may lack the flexibility necessary for successful decision making.

Observation 2

As volume decreases, costs tend to become proportionately more fixed. However, the converse is true as volume increases, which can lead to improper use of costs in decision making. For example, a firm which decides to accept a special order at variable cost may be dismayed to find that the increased production required additional resources (such as another supervisor), which previously had been treated as fixed and, therefore, ignored in pricing. However, this example does not show that separation of fixed and variable costs is wrong, only that the separation can be done poorly. Clearly, if managers focus only on fixed versus variable costs at one level of production in making a decision about the costs of another level of production, they may make bad decisions. The management accountant should focus on the future — what will costs be at the increased (or decreased) level of output. The need for the additional supervisor would have been seen and included in the additional cost of the special order. Incremental costs are important here — and incremental does not necessarily equal variable.

Observation 3

Fixed and variable cost classification can be fluid. A fixed cost in one context may be variable in another. For example, in an advertising agency, creative time is variable from the standpoint of an individual account but fixed for the agency as a whole.

Observation 4

Many costs are neither entirely fixed nor entirely variable — they are semivariable. They require the use of statistical methods and historical data to separate the fixed from the variable components. If semivariable costs represent an immaterial proportion of the total, they can be arbitrarily assigned to fixed or variable categories, or even ignored, with little impact on decision making. However, semivariable costs (for example, energy costs — which have a fixed billing component as well as a variable usage component) have come to represent a growing portion of the total. Hence, companies must deal with them more carefully or risk making incorrect decisions.

Observation 5

Labor costs, which have traditionally been treated as strictly variable, are becoming more fixed in nature. Union contracts, internal company regulations, government policies (for example, unemployment insurance taxes, which are based in part on a company's stable employment history) are some of the factors leading to at least some fixed component of labor cost. Decision makers who treat this cost as totally variable may well be misled.

All of these concerns regarding use of fixed and variable costs have some validity. As with any management accounting tool, the key is to be thoroughly familiar with the technique and its potential pitfalls as well as its promised rewards.

The Impact of High Technology on Cost Classification

The "high tech challenge" to management accounting was addressed by Littrell (1984). He stressed the importance of adjusting management accounting techniques to the relevant stage of the product life cycle. Since high tech firms are constantly innovating, they frequently market products in the introduction and growth stages — as opposed to the mature stage — of the product life cycle. Accountants must recognize the impact of these stages on costs. For example, capacity changes lead to movement of the relevant range in cost-volume-profit analysis and difficulty in applying fixed overhead to units of production. The distinction between fixed and variable costs blurs as cost becomes a continuum. The result is that the common assumptions about linear cost (and revenue) behavior become less tenable and many costs become semivariable.

Seed (1984) also proposed changes in cost accounting to accommodate changing technology and the age of robotics. First, management accountants should reexamine the direct/indirect cost classification. Previously, the term direct was a synonym for variable while indirect was thought of as a synonym for fixed; these equivalencies no longer hold. Second, companies should shift their emphasis from cost operating centers to investment and inventory management control. Finally, equipment costs should be assigned to producing departments on the basis of fair rental value. Especially with the advent of highly computerized and mechanized firms, fixed costs have increased dramatically with a concomitant decrease in variable costs. Reliance on direct and indirect cost classifications can cause firms to overlook the higher breakeven points, increased profit margins, and return on investment which characterize firms in the age of robotics.

Examples of Fixed and Variable Cost Usage

In this section, five examples of fixed and variable cost separation and use are described. These examples include profitability analysis of advertising agency accounts, regression analysis of overhead incurred by aerospace contractors, fixed and variable cost identification by hospitals, maintenance of a high proportion of variable costs in a data processing department, and use of fixed and variable cost data in pricing. While the focus is specific, implications can be drawn from each which can benefit a broader cross section of businesses.

Advertising Agency Accounting

Mills (1983) gives a good example of the role fixed and variable costs play in instituting financial discipline in an advertising agency. A major loss led to the discovery of serious flaws in the agency's cost accounting system. Specifically, the cost accounting system could track costs and revenues for the agency as a whole but could not do so for individual accounts. "Some accounts were highly profitable and others extremely unprofitable, but top management had no idea which were which." (p.47)

The key to the solution was to institute a system of cost control by account. The only variable cost of the advertising agency was employee time; all other costs (for example, rent, utilities) were fixed and lumped together as overhead. In consultation with the American Association of Advertising Agencies, the firm developed a system of forecasting billings, revenues, and costs for each account for a one-year period. Actual costs and revenues could then be compared with the forecasted amounts. On an individual basis, all employees kept time sheets listing the time spent on each account during the day. The variable cost per account was then calculated by multiplying cost per employee times the fraction of time spent on the account and then summing.

Using these methods, the agency was able to ensure that revenues at least covered variable costs and contributed to fixed costs. Accounts likely to yield a loss could be identified early, allowing management to determine if the account should be dropped or if special considerations merited taking a loss (for example, expected future profitability or account prestige likely to bring in more business). Separation and use of fixed and variable costs for planning and control led to profitability one year after implementation (1982), even in a time of general economic decline.

Aerospace

Gross and Dienemann (1978) developed a series of models which analyzed overhead costs for ten aerospace industry contractors for the period 1968-1974. A series of regression equations were estimated with annual overhead costs as a function of direct labor and materials costs for the year as well as direct costs and overhead costs for the prior year. Total overhead was divided into a number of categories including: indirect labor, employee benefits, payroll tax, communications, travel, production related, land and buildings, facilities and equipment, administrative and future business, and all other overhead. Regression equations were run for each of these categories; an important result was that no category of overhead was found to be fixed. All categories varied to some degree with the level of direct costs. For example, even physical facilities were variable (land and buildings approximately 33% variable and facilities and equipment 66% variable).

Gross and Dienemann (1978) concluded that predictive equations for corporate overhead costs in the aerospace industry can be developed and that they predict future costs reasonably well. They believe this initial success justifies continued contractor reporting of overhead cost.

Hospitals

The importance of fixed and variable cost identification for hospitals was discussed by Nagy (1982). The advent of Diagnosis Related Group (DRG)-based reimbursement by the government and the emphasis on cost reduction by health insurance firms has led to the need for careful cost analysis by hospitals. Nagy used managerial judgment as the method of cost separation. He described various types of hospital costs, organizing them into the following categories: committed fixed costs (for example, management salaries), discretionary fixed costs (for example, travel and meeting expenses), pure variable costs (for example, medical supplies and physicians' fees), and step variable costs (such as . . . equipment repair, other medical personnel salaries, office supplies).

The article provided a good description of the chosen cost categories and showed how they could be applied to the hospital situation. Managerial accounting techniques which use fixed and variable costs as input were suggested briefly.

Data Processing

Mintz (1978) presented information on the way data processing (DP) departments could use fixed and variable cost information to maintain an efficient, low-cost operation. In general, the objective of this article was to classify typical data processing costs as being fixed, variable, or semivariable. Mintz notes that many DP center costs are step variable. That is, the costs are fixed for a relatively small range of activity, then they jump up abruptly and stay fixed for another range of activity (for example, additions to computing "core"). He advises that such costs should be structured such that the "risers" in the stair-step-like ascent be as shallow as possible in order to approximate a variable cost closely. For example, he suggests that DP managers maintain flexibility by not making long-term commitments for computer equipment — perhaps by taking advantage of timesharing.

Specific suggestions regarding ways to keep costs approximately variable include: utilizing service bureaus for specific tasks (for example, payroll processing), utilizing timesharing services, and adding I/O devices and core to temporarily upgrade capacity. The objective in each case is to maintain sufficient flexibility so that increases and decreases in volume can be adjusted to with relative ease.

Application to Pricing

The role of fixed and variable costs in pricing was discussed by Keegan (1984), who advocated a "paragon" pricing method. Paragon pricing is a cost-based concept meant to provide direction to management in setting the actual market price. The paragon price is a "revenue amount which reflects the costs of the item plus a margin in excess of those costs — set by policy — which provides an adequate return on capital. It is a long-term concept, the benchmark upon which to determine shorter-term price or product strategy." (p. 25)

The issue of concern here is what costs are to be considered in setting the paragon price. Keegan advocated the use of full costs because of the long-term nature of this construct. However, he recognized the importance of variable costs in responding to special market situations. In other words, paragon pricing is to be used as a compass, to provide direction. It is not to be applied rigidly but, rather, tempered by knowledge of market conditions and used in conjunction with fixed and variable cost information. For example, a company would use knowledge of variable costs to set a survival price in economic downturns. This survival price must at least cover variable costs incurred at the reduced volume level. Keegan also reinforced the point that as volume decreases, some variable costs tend to become fixed. This must be recognized in setting the survival price.

Three Assessments of Fixed and Variable Cost Use

Three surveys of firms' usage of fixed and variable costs have been undertaken. The first was done by the National Association of Accountants in 1980. It examined the extent, purpose, and use of fixed and variable costs by firms. The second survey, Govindarajan and Anthony (1983), was much more narrowly focused. It examined firms' pricing policies. The results contradicted those reported by the NAA. The third study, Bruegelmann et al. (1985), examined the use of variable costing in pricing decisions.

The NAA (1980) report (*Management Uses of Fixed and Variable Expense Analysis*) presented the findings of a survey of 800 wholesale-retail and manufacturing firms. Of the 29.1% of the firms which responded, approximately two-thirds indicated that they used fixed and variable expense analysis at least to some extent. Because so few wholesale-retail firms sampled used fixed and variable costs, results were reported only for the manufacturing firms.

A variety of methods were reported for separating costs into fixed and variable components for cost-volume-profit analysis. By far the most popular method was managerial judgment. About 81.6% of the firms used this method at least half the time. By way of contrast, 36.7% of the firms used engineering and/or work measurement studies, and 19.2% used statistically based techniques at least half the time.

The primary uses of fixed and variable expense analysis were found to be management planning and reporting. This type of analysis also was used to an extent in specific decision making and to an even lesser extent in evaluation of management performance. It was also found that large companies (defined as having sales of more than $50 million) were more likely to use fixed and variable expenses analysis than small companies.

Other questions related to length of the time horizon, cost behavior assumptions, and use of fixed and variable costs in external reporting. In general, the time horizon was less than four years, costs were assumed to be linear, and virtually no external reporting of fixed and variable costs occurred.

Of special interest is the question which asks whether fixed and variable costs are used in product pricing decisions. Respondents were asked to indicate the frequency with which expenses are formally identified as fixed or variable, as an aid in managerial planning or decision making . . . (for) product pricing decisions. A majority of the sample, 71.4%, indicated that costs are formally divided into fixed and variable components for this purpose at least half the time. Another 17.6% indicated they use these breakdowns for pricing occasionally (less than half the time). Thus, 89% of these manufacturing firms use fixed and variable expenses in pricing at least some of the time.

Diametrically opposite results were reported by Govindarajan and Anthony (1983), hereinafter G-A. They conducted a survey of the Fortune 1,000 industrial companies (response rate of 50.5%) regarding the use of cost data in pricing decisions. Respondents checked which one of the five pricing formulas (for example, based on variable cost of production, full cost of production) best described the way their firms used cost data in arriving at a selling price for a typical product. Of those responding, only 17% indicated the use of variable costing. G-A concluded that most companies use full costs rather than variable costs, implying that firms do not separate costs along fixed and variable lines for pricing purposes.

Bruegelmann et al. (1985) conducted in-person interviews with a small sample of company executives responsible for pricing. This more flexible format enabled the researchers to elicit a great deal of information about the way companies handle pricing in a wide variety of situations. Bruegelmann et al. concluded that although firms generally use full cost as the basis for routine pricing decisions, variable costs are regularly used to set prices in short-term situations.

In all probability, the NAA (1980) and Bruegelmann et al. (1985) studies more accurately described companies' usage of fixed and variable costs in pricing decisions. The more general phrasing of the NAA question allowed firms to indicate use, but not exclusive use, of fixed and variable costs in the pricing decision across all product lines. Bruegelmann et al. concentrated on the characteristics of the situation which might call for reliance on variable costs. G-A, on the other hand, concentrated on the format of the eventual pricing calculation for one "typical" product.

Conclusion

A review of the literature shows the complexity of fixed and variable cost classification and usage. It is clear that this methodology can be fraught with both potential pitfalls for the unwary user and rewards for the thinking decision maker. This literature can be divided into two sections — one outlining cost separation methods and the other discussing fixed and variable cost uses.

Fixed and variable cost separation has not received much attention in the accounting press. One usually infers from articles that fixed and variable costs are identified through the use of managerial judgment. Some articles (for example, those by Nagy, 1982 and Mintz, 1978) do provide assistance in determining cost classification by giving specific examples of fixed, variable, and semivariable costs common to particular industries.

The article by Gross and Dienemann (1978), detailing cost separation by ordinary least squares, is unusual in accounting oriented journals; such separation methodologies can be found more frequently in industrial engineering journals.

The use of fixed and variable costs in management accounting applications has been discussed more frequently. Fixed and variable costs, properly considered and tailored for the specific purpose the user has in mind, can be an extremely powerful and flexible tool for decision making. Just the process of classifying costs according to their behavior forces the decision maker to become more familiar with the underlying cost structure.

Chapters 5 to 7 examine management accountants in the "real world." They take us from the world of books and articles to actual application of fixed and variable costs.

Chapter 5

Survey Methodology and Results

Introduction

The preceding chapter used information gleaned from journal articles and textbooks to show how companies *should* separate fixed and variable costs. Another approach involves finding out just how firms handle the problem in actual practice. In order to investigate the actual behavior of firms, a survey of companies was conducted. The purpose was to move from the "how to" of textbooks to a description of corporate management accounting behavior.

While there has been a previous survey of firms' use of fixed and variable costs (NAA, 1980), it yielded general information. For example, the study found that 89% of manufacturing firms surveyed use fixed and variable costs in pricing at least some of the time, and about 82% use managerial judgment to separate fixed from variable costs. That information is interesting and indicates how widespread the use of this technique is. By extension, it provides a feel for the degree to which companies value fixed and variable cost analysis (that is, the more firms use it, the more valuable it must be).

The survey designed and conducted for this study sought to advance and extend the previous work. The goal was to probe further — asking why, how, and what problems were encountered in using fixed and variable cost analysis. In short, it was meant to flesh out the numbers garnered previously. The survey consisted of a series of guided conversations with management accountants and financial executives on the subject of fixed and variable costs. In conducting the survey, anecdotal material was welcomed. Therefore, the results do not lend themselves to tabular presentation; they are best reported in narrative fashion.

This chapter first presents the survey methodology and a description of the survey instrument. Next, answers to the survey questions are reviewed. Finally, some general conclusions and implications for other firms are drawn.

Methodology

Survey Objectives

Because of the nature of the information desired, it was decided that telephone interviews and face-to-face interviews would be more appropriate than a mail questionnaire. One can obtain more in-depth information from telephone and personal interviews than from written questionnaires. In addition, respondents are much more likely to relate valuable information when they interact with an interviewer. Therefore, in order to make it as easy as possible for respondents to relate examples from their experiences, the survey was designed to be conducted either via telephone or in person.

The Sample

Survey participants were obtained from 25 companies. For the most part, the respondents were controllers or chief financial officers of their company. Table 3 gives characteristics of the companies participating in the survey.

A convenience sample was used. Because this was not a random sample, no statistical inferences can be made. Instead, the sample was constructed to find out how a variety of firms employ fixed and variable costs so that others who are interested in this topic can see what is being done. Potential respondents were chosen such that a broad cross section of companies was represented. Firms representing manufacturing, services, construction, retailing, the nonprofit sector, and regulated industries were included in the sample. Sales for the most recent fiscal year ranged from $100,000 to $34 billion. The firms were selected on the basis that they used fixed and variable costs. A deliberate effort was made to locate firms which separate costs into fixed and variable components and use those costs in decision making.

The Interview

Telephone interviews were conducted with respondents. On average, the actual interview took 15 minutes. Six interviews were conducted in person at the respondent's place of business. These

Table 3
CHARACTERISTICS OF SURVEY PARTICIPANTS

Characteristic	Number of Firms (n = 25)
Net Sales Revenue for Most Recent Fiscal Year:	
Less than $5,000,000	9
$5,000,000-$100,000,000	7
More than $100,000,000	9
Industry by SIC* Division:	
C. Construction	1
D. Manufacturing	15
E. Transportation, Communications, Electric, Gas, and Sanitary Services	4
G. Retail Trade	1
I. Services	4
Title of Respondent:	
Controller/Assistant Controller	9
Treasurer	2
President	2
Other Financial	8
CPA Consultant	4

*Standard Industrial Classification Manual, U.S. Government Printing Office, Office of Management and Budget, 1972.

lasted approximately one hour each. In all cases, answers to the questionnaire (see the Appendix) provided the interview structure. In only one case was the questionnaire completed by mail.

Results of the Survey

Results of the survey are briefly presented in the order in which the questions were asked. A longer discussion of some answers is reserved for the discussion which follows.

General Use of Fixed and Variable Costs

Survey participants were asked if their companies' management used fixed and variable cost classifications for: planning, reporting, decision making, evaluation, or other. Planning and decision making were the categories cited most often with 15 companies choosing each. Only five of the 25 companies used fixed and variable costs for reporting purposes, although ten said they did use them in evaluation — which meant profitability analysis to most. No other general categories were cited.

Formal Reports to Management

Nine companies reported fixed and variable expense classifications on regular reports to management. The reports took a variety of forms. Four firms compiled periodic internal financial statements using a direct costing format. These were later converted to an absorption basis through an inventory adjustment (see Case Study One for an extended example). Two others, subsidiaries of large companies, sent monthly operating expense and analysis reports citing fixed and variable costs incurred to corporate headquarters. A public utility noted that fixed and variable cost information was provided routinely to the regulatory commission. Two companies which did not show fixed and variable costs on management reports indicated they could do so easily.

Specific Purposes for Using Fixed and Variable Costs

The specific purposes for which firms used fixed and variable costs are shown in Table 4. The most frequently cited uses were for budgeting and pricing (48% of firms used the approach for these purposes). The next most frequently cited reasons were for profitability analysis, for existing products (40%), and for profitability analysis of new products (28%). The frequency of companies citing pricing as a reason was probably artificially low because four firms in the sample were cost centers and, of course, they do not set prices.

Who Decides How to Separate Cost?

Controllers were most frequently cited as the individuals who decided how costs were to be divided into fixed and variable components. Twenty-four percent of the firms (a total of six) left that responsibility to the cost accounting department in conjunction with line personnel. Outside CPAs and finance departments made the decision for two firms apiece. The budgeting manager, economics department, and engineering department were each cited once.

Method of Cost Separation

The overwhelmingly favorite method of cost separation was mana-

Table 4
SPECIFIC PURPOSES FOR WHICH FIRMS USE
FIXED AND VARIABLE COSTS

Purpose	Number of Citations*
Budgeting	12
Capital Expenditures	3
Special Orders	3
Variance Analysis	5
Direct Costing	4
Breakeven Analysis	5
Pricing	12
Profitability Analysis— New Products	7
Profitability Analysis— Existing Products	10
Other	1

*Number of citations totals more than 25 because some firms cited more than one purpose.

gerial judgment. Eighty percent of the companies employed it. As a basis for judgment, one respondent noted that his firm relied on trade publications and outside charts and data. This firm is in the aviation industry and fuel usage is its primary variable cost. It was able to find material on fuel usage by particular types of aircraft in aviation journals. Three companies opted for statistical methods, and one chose an engineering approach. Of the statistics users, two employed ordinary least squares and one analyzed costs using a combination of scattergraphs and regression analysis.

Classification of the Chart of Accounts

Question six dealt with the classification of the companies' accounts as strictly fixed or strictly variable. Thirty-two percent of the firms reported using this method, although one qualified its answer by saying "somewhat," indicating a less formal separation. The account classification systems of these firms had been in place from one to 20 years with most (five) for five years or less. Thus, these systems are relatively recent and most have not been updated since their inception. Two firms update formally on an annual basis; the others indicated that changes are made when the need arises.

Recognition of Semivariable Costs

The majority of firms (64%) did not recognize any costs as

semivariable or mixed. Five firms which did recognize the existence of semivariable costs went on to say that either they did not know what to do with them or they arbitrarily assigned them to strictly fixed or strictly variable categories. The remaining four firms separated semivariable costs.

Bases for Describing Variable Costs

A variety of bases were used to describe variable costs. Forty-four percent of the firms used dollars per unit produced. Those units included: hours of professional time, pounds of chemicals, greeting cards, patient days, laboratory tests, automobiles, newspapers, and hours of flying time. Other bases included dollars per machine hour (cited by two firms) and dollars per labor hour (cited by six firms). Bases used by one firm each were dollars per: barrel of throughput, dollar of capital investment, kilowatt hour, and sales dollars. Six firms did not relate variable costs to an independent base.

Relevant Range for Cost Relationships

The question regarding the relevant range within which cost relationships hold constant was adapted from the NAA (1980) survey. The concept of the relevant range led to misunderstanding then and the situation did not clear up significantly here. The results will be reported here and expanded upon in the discussion section. Most respondents (60%) had no idea what the boundaries of the relevant range were for their firms. Two firms, on the other hand, were quite specific, both, coincidentally, citing a 15% change in fixed cost. Others described their relevant ranges as very sensitive (two firms), not very sensitive (five firms), and somewhat sensitive (one firm). Five firms noted that the relevant range was tied to the physical size of their current plant.

Length of the Short Run

The length of the short-run period was perceived to be one year for 16 firms. Others noted time periods of five years, three years, two months, and one month.

For most, the length of the short-run time period did not vary with the type of cost. Only five companies cited the use of more than one short-run period. A flight training school and charter service tied length of the short run to the economic life of an airplane — which was two to three years for pilot training but indefinite for charter service. A construction company representative related the importance of economic conditions to the short run. She noted that fixed assets wear out more quickly in a boom. Still others noted that buildings typically have a longer short-run period than other assets.

Informal Use of Fixed and Variable Costing

The sample was split on informal use of fixed and variable cost information. Forty-eight percent of the firms said, "no," it was not used, however, several of those were firms which use a direct costing system, hence their usage is formal. Of the 13 firms (52%) reporting informal use, differential costing, special orders, and planning were cited most often as uses for fixed and variable costs.

Would Firms Like More Use of Fixed and Variable Costs?

When asked if they would like to see more use of fixed and variable costing in their firms, 60% said, "no," and ten (40%) said, "yes." The latter wanted to see more use for pricing, periodic segment operations reporting, and the implementation of a manufacturing requirements plan. One respondent noted that fixed and variable costing is a "fantastic vehicle for cost control." A hospital controller pointed out that new methods of reimbursement are forcing hospitals into using fixed and variable costs, and that the hospital was engaged in radically expanding its management accounting system to account for them.

Factors Influencing Appropriateness of Fixed and Variable Costs

Question 13 originated from the preliminary interviews undertaken before the survey instrument was finalized. A management accountant mentioned that the direct costing system worked well for some plants but not for others. Specifically, he felt a direct costing system could not be implemented in a plant with many products because joint cost allocation became a problem. Hence, the question, "Do you think that the appropriateness of fixed and variable cost breakdowns depends on particular factors?" Interestingly, another accountant, from the same industry as the one cited above, believed the breakdown to be crucial in plants with many products — in order to ensure that each makes a contribution to fixed cost and profit. Three respondents cited firm size as an important factor. As one put it, small companies just starting out need to use fixed and variable costing more than established companies because "as a company approaches maturity it can absorb a few hits." One felt it would be more applicable to process costing than job-order costing. Five listed other factors such as the nature of the distribution process, the amount of unused plant capacity, and the conceptual sophistication of other people in the company.

Value to External Parties

Question 14 asked whether or not respondents thought information on fixed and variable costs would be of value to external parties and if they currently provide such information. Eighty-four percent thought information on fixed and variable costs would be of no value to external parties. One mentioned "bankers (were) slow in switching their thinking" from absorption to direct costing. Four respondents thought this information would be useful. Paradoxically, one felt that bankers understood fixed and variable costs; she felt that providing such information in the form of breakeven analysis had led to more favorable loan consideration for her firm. Three other respondents pointed out that investors might be interested in the level of fixed versus variable expense in order to do a qualitative breakeven analysis. *Only one* company has provided fixed and variable cost information to external parties, and that was to the bank as part of a loan application. All others did not provide it. One respondent said emphatically that he would not do this. He noted that he spent a considerable amount of time amassing fixed and variable cost information and that he did not want that information to leak out to his competitors.

Discussion

The survey resulted in a number of important observations and potentially useful insights. These may be grouped under six headings: the incorporation of fixed and variable costs into the firm's formal reporting system, the method of cost separation, the classification of account titles according to cost behavior, the relevant range, examples of fixed and variable costs, and some uses of fixed and variable costs encountered in practice.

Formal Versus Informal Use of Fixed and Variable Costs

The use of fixed and variable costs was pervasive in these 25 companies' decision making. Some incorporated fixed and variable cost breakdowns in the formal reporting system. Naturally, this occurred for the four companies using a direct costing system, but it also occurred for a number of other companies which must submit periodic operating reports to corporate headquarters with costs broken down into fixed and variable components. Even more frequently, though, fixed and variable costs were used informally. All respondents were able to quickly list the fixed and variable costs faced by their companies. There were even a few occasions when a respondent said his or her firm really did not use fixed and variable costs and then went on to categorize a business segment in terms of covering its variable costs and contributing to fixed overhead. Clearly, the concept was being used, albeit not consciously in all cases.

Method of Separating Fixed and Variable Costs

The cost separation method used by 80% of the firms surveyed was managerial judgment. There was no obvious relationship between size of firm and use of statistical methods. The four which used statistical methods or engineering studies included small, medium, and large firms, reporting revenue ranging from $3 million to $972 million. They represented three different SIC industrial divisions. Thus, it is difficult to delineate the factors which encourage firms to choose one methodology over another. It may result simply from the different preferences or training of the controllers in the various companies. Also, some respondents said that the high cost of sophisticated methodology was not worth the purported benefits.

It appears that managerial judgment is used more to assign costs to fixed or variable categories (for example, one company sees wages, rent, and depreciation as fixed and raw materials as variable) than to separate a semivariable cost into fixed and variable components. Utilities expense was especially troublesome to several companies; it was perceived as semivariable and was becoming a larger proportion of total cost. Yet, these companies did not separate the semivariable costs for utilities into fixed and variable components. This failure to separate fixed and variable utilities expense was due to the belief that managerial judgment was not adequate for the task and that other methods were too difficult to use.

The Chart of Accounts

One might expect that companies which use fixed and variable costs would set up the chart of accounts according to cost behavior. However, for the most part, companies have developed their cost reporting systems in response to financial accounting needs and then adapted them as necessary to provide the data needed for management decision making. While eight firms did report classifying account titles as fixed or variable, only one reported setting up the accounts to reflect cost-volume relationships. That person, a controller for a small manufacturing firm, had been requested by corporate headquarters to separate costs into fixed and variable components. He studied historical data for each cost putting a fair amount of effort into cost separation of even semivariable costs. Headquarters responded that it did not want that level of detail. Instead, he was asked simply to classify each account as strictly fixed or strictly variable. He did so, after rearranging the accounts such that each one contained only fixed or variable costs.

It should be noted that several respondents, whose firms did not formally classify account titles as fixed or variable, did think of them in that way. For example, two respondents pulled out copies of their most recent income statements and ticked off expense categories as variable or fixed. Another did the same thing using a cost of goods manufactured schedule.

The Relevant Range

The concept of relevant range is a fairly subtle one. Theoretically, the relevant range represents the level(s) of activity over which cost relationships remain constant. That is, if volume increases (decreases), fixed costs stay fixed and variable costs increase (decrease). Some respondents intuitively related the relevant range to the size of the physical plant. For example, a retailer said he was relatively happy in his present location. To substantially increase volume, he would have to move to larger quarters or start up a second store. However, if volume decreased, he could remain in his present location. So, his relevant range was from $0 to somewhat more than his current $140,000 annual sales, and was relatively insensitive to volume changes. Still another respondent, from a large manufacturing firm, recognized a relevant range which was sensitive to volume changes; an increase or decrease of 15% would result in changed fixed cost. Another respondent noted that increased activity required more maintenance on machinery and that the cost-volume relationship changed because "maintenance generates maintenance." In other words, routine maintenance on heavy machinery was tied to the number of hours used. As production increased, machine hours increased, leading to more routine maintenance. This was a straightforward variable cost situation. However, the more often maintenance workers dealt with the machinery, the more likely that mistakes would be made which would require correction, that is, even more maintenance and repair. It was still a variable cost relationship but the variable rate did not remain constant.

In the relevant range, fixed costs remain constant despite changes in volume. This factor can lead to problems when fixed costs are treated, in effect, as variable, as in the application of fixed overhead to units of production under full costing. A utilities industry executive referred to the "death spiral," in which fewer sales mean that there is less volume over which to spread fixed costs, leading to higher rates for reduced usage. Taken to its absurd conclusion, eventually one kilowatt hour would bear the entire fixed cost of production. In another example of the death spiral, a few years ago, a large manufacturer of computer equipment found that one of its plants was failing. The problem was a combination of productive inefficiency and rigid transfer pricing rules (that all intracompany transfers take place at full cost). Because the plant was somewhat inefficient, its full cost was undercut by the corporation's competitors. Other plants within the corporation began to purchase the component from the competition, leaving the original plant with reduced volume and a smaller base over which to spread fixed costs. In an effort to save the plant, the corporation has permitted a deviation from full-cost transfer price to a market-based transfer price. The final outcome remains to be seen.

Firms which lease assets may find that the relevant range shifts, depending on the care the lessors take with those assets. The economic lives of automobiles, for example, depend to an extent on how hard they are driven. Thus, the length of the short run and the breadth of the relevant range may be at least partially beyond the control of a company.

A large manufacturing company with a number of plants defined fixed cost as the cost which would occur at zero production. The financial administrator of one of those plants saw the definition as irrelevant to decision making since it could never occur. His company has never let a plant sit idle for a year (its planning period). He further explained that the fixed costs at zero production were subtracted from total annual costs to obtain total variable costs. Then total costs and total variable costs were compared across plants in order to evaluate performance. This practice makes little sense.

Variable costs figured in this way are not necessarily variable because the fixed costs calculated were not those for actual production but, instead, represented fixed costs for zero production. This definition of fixed cost is an economist's definition. Management accountants would not use that definition because it ignores the relevant range. They recognize that the amount of fixed costs at one level of production do not necessarily equal the amount of fixed costs at some other level of production.

Examples of Fixed and Variable Costs

In cost accounting textbooks, it is traditional to categorize direct materials and direct labor as strictly variable. All other costs must be examined on a case-by-case basis. In reality, there appears to be no cost which can be indisputably classified as variable or fixed. Instead, a fixed cost for one firm may be variable for another. For example, several petrochemical firms noted that all costs other than throughput (the raw material) were fixed — including labor. Respondents from these firms felt that certain other costs might be variable but these were considered immaterial. On the other hand, a job order manufacturer of heavy duty components for oil refineries said his labor costs were variable. Despite the fact that he runs a union shop, he can hire and lay off employees with relative ease. Surprisingly, all other costs for this company (except for depreciation and rent) were considered variable as well, although some costs "varied more than others."

It might be expected that inventory in a retail store is a variable cost. Not true, said one retailer of women's specialty clothing. For this small company, clothing inventory was viewed as a fixed cost because once an order is made it cannot be cancelled and unsold items cannot be returned to the manufacturer.

Some Uses of Fixed and Variable Costs

The accountant for a greeting card manufacturer described the difficulties she faced in figuring the breakeven point. The firm creates six different cards, each requiring different amounts (and costs) of materials and labor. Because of incomplete records, she was unable to accurately determine the variable cost for each type of card. The solution was to combine the six varieties into one "average" card for which an average variable cost could be calculated. A further discussion of this situation is presented in Case Study Two.

The above solution would not work for certain other products. In buying and leasing heavy machinery, for example, the breakeven point has to be figured separately for each asset because of differing lives and warranties. In a similar vein, a manufacturer of hand-held tools developed a method of relating machine set up costs to lot sizes. While a cost accounting textbook would recommend standard economic order quantity techniques to figure the optimal size production run, this company realized that tracking fixed and variable costs by run size was necessary because the relevant range can shift as lot size changes.

A newspaper publishing company representative would like to see fixed and variable costs used more frequently in pricing, especially in setting circulation rates and advertising lineage rates. As it stands now, this company does use its knowledge of fixed and variable costs to quote prices for an advertiser who wants to insert a supplement. The production department determines a price quote by breaking out the incremental cost of the supplement and adding some predetermined profit.

In another pricing application, a certified public accountant noted that he considers cost in "value pricing." For example, suppose a client calls with an unusual question which the accountant cannot answer. The accountant will spend time researching that question and then bill the client — but not for the entire amount of time. Instead, part of that time is temporarily absorbed by the CPA as "educational investment." Then later, if a second client asks the same question, the CPA does not answer immediately and bill the client for five minutes of professional time. Rather, he bills a somewhat higher amount in order to realize a return on the fixed cost of the previous investment in education.

A final note should be made regarding the interrelationship of variable costs and pricing. For many firms, volume means profit. However, as one respondent pointed out, "if the product is underpriced (that is, priced below variable costs) and usage increases, it would have a devastating effect."

Several firms demonstrated interesting applications of fixed and variable cost analysis. These are discussed at length in the next section.

Chapter 6

Three Case Studies

Some of the firms surveyed used extensive fixed and variable costing procedures. Three of these are detailed here, using simplified examples. Case Study One presents the direct costing system of a large petrochemical company. Case Study Two describes the way a greeting card manufacturer used fixed and variable costs for breakeven analysis. Case Study Three includes the use of fixed and variable cost separation in a not-for-profit hospital. Petrochem, Caralot Cards, and MedCenter, the names devised for the companies in these cases, are fictitious in order to preserve the anonymity of the actual companies on which the three studies are based.

Case Study One

This case study presents a simplified version of the standard direct costing system of Petrochem, a large petrochemical manufacturer. Standard costs for this firm are classified as fixed and variable. Actual fixed and variable costs then are compared with standard costs on a monthly basis. Price and efficiency variances are computed as part of the ongoing performance evaluation system. Finally, an inventory adjustment is made in order to convert direct costs to full costs for financial reporting purposes.

Assume for purposes of this example:

1. There is one location which produces a planned volume of one product, chemex, at a budgeted cost. The plant is responsible for noting price variances and for explaining all efficiency and fixed cost variances.
2. Corporate headquarters consists of the marketing and administration departments. These departments have no variable costs.

3. One accounting period is shown, the start-up period. It begins on January 1 of Year 1.
4. Only the finished product is inventoried. LIFO is used for tax and financial accounting purposes, so costs to be inventoried are based on December costs.
5. Variable costs for the plant consist of raw materials, processing supplies, and utilities. All other costs are fixed. (Managerial judgment was the method used to classify these costs.)
6. In Year 1, 10,000,000 lbs. of chemex were sold at $.50/lb.; 11,000,000 lbs. were produced using 11,100,000 lbs. of raw material. Standard variable cost was $.25/lb. of final product.

Exhibit 1 shows the planned and actual fixed costs for headquarters. A favorable variance of $30,000 has been computed.

Exhibit 1
HEADQUARTERS COST SUMMARY — ALL COSTS FIXED
FOR THE PERIOD ENDING 12/31/YEAR 1
(IN $000s)

	Budget	Actual	Variance
Marketing	160	150	10
Administration	120	100	20
Total Headquarters	280	250	30

Planned and actual costs for the plant are shown in Exhibits 2 and 3. Exhibit 2 presents variable costs which consist of raw materials, processing supplies (catalyst and dye), and utilities. Actual variable costs of $3,200,000 were $450,000 above budgeted costs for 11,000,000 lbs. of chemex produced.

Exhibit 2
PLANT VARIABLE COST REPORT
FOR THE PERIOD ENDING 12/31/YEAR 1
(IN $000s)

	Budget	Actual	Variance
Raw Materials	2,623	3,000	(377)
Processing Supplies:			
Catalyst	22	50	(28)
Dye	17	20	(3)
Utilities	88	130	(42)
Total Plant Variable Cost	2,750	3,200	(450)

Exhibit 3
PLANT FIXED COST REPORT
FOR THE PERIOD ENDING 12/31/YEAR 1
(IN $000s)

	Budget	Actual	Variance
Operations	1,150	1,090	60
Labor	100	110	(10)
Total Plant Fixed Cost	1,250	1,200	50

Exhibit 3 shows planned and actual fixed costs for chemex production. Labor and all other costs are assumed to be fixed. Again, a variance (of $50,000 favorable) is computed.

Exhibit 4 tracks the inventories of raw materials and finished product in pounds. Exhibit 5 details variable input usage and its impact on inventory in dollars.

Exhibit 4
VOLUME STOCK BALANCE
FOR THE PERIOD ENDING 12/31/YEAR 1
(IN $000s)

	Charge Stock/ Production	Purchases	Sales	1/1	Inventories 12/31	Change
Raw Material	11,100	11,000	—	—	—	—
Chemex	11,000		10,000	—	1,000	1,000

Exhibit 5
DOLLAR VALUE STOCK BALANCE
FOR THE PERIOD ENDING 12/31/YEAR 1
(IN $000s)

	Charge Stock/ Production	Purchases	Sales	1/1	Inventories 12/31	Change
Input:						
Raw Material	3,000	3,000				
Processing Supplies and Utilities	200	200				
Total Inputs	3,200	3,200				
Output:						
Chemex	2,750		2,500	—	250	250
Variable Variance	(450)					

The inventory adjustment computation necessary to convert direct costs to full costs is shown in Exhibit 6. Full costs of $.40/lb. of chemex are calculated by dividing total production cost (variable cost plus fixed cost) by pounds produced. Then standard direct cost per pound (total budgeted direct costs from Exhibit 2 divided by pounds produced) of $.25 is subtracted from $.40 and the result multiplied by the increase in inventory to obtain the inventory adjustment figure.

Exhibit 6
INVENTORY ADJUSTMENT COMPUTATION
FOR THE PERIOD ENDING 12/31/YEAR 1
(IN $000s)

	1/1 Balance		Change		12/31 Balance	
	Volume	$	Volume	$/lb.	Volume	$
Chemex	—	—	1,000	.40*	1,000	400
Less:						
Standard Direct Cost			1,000	.25**	1,000	(250)
Inventory Adjustment						150

*Full Cost Per Lb. ($3,200 + $1,200)/(11,000) = $.40
**Standard Direct Cost Per Lb. ($2,750/11,000) = $.25

A Profit Center Summary Report is shown in Exhibit 7. It is set up in income statement format and is based on a flexible budget for actual production. Direct manufacturing costs are shown first, then they are adjusted to full cost via the inventory adjustment. Plant and headquarters fixed costs are shown in terms of their impact on gross margin and operating income. Planning and actual operating income can be compared and corrective action taken.

The standard direct costing system was used by Petrochem for both planning and control. During formal budgeting for the next year, a process which spanned six months, Petrochem would devise a projected Profit Center Summary similar to Exhibit 7. If the projected operating income did not provide sufficient return on investment, budgeted costs and revenues would be revised until the targeted rate of return was achieved.

In the control phase, the Profit Center Summary of Exhibit 7 spotlighted deviations of actual amounts from budget figures. While only one product was used in this case study, in reality, this firm produced many products. Variable costs were accumulated for each product and reported in Individual Product Analyses. Individuals

Exhibit 7
PROFIT CENTER SUMMARY
FOR THE PERIOD ENDING 12/31/YEAR 1
(IN $000s)

	Volume		Net Revenue		Direct Cost		Gross Margin	
	Budget	Actual	Budget	Actual	Budget	Actual	Budget	Actual
Chemex:								
Domestic		9,000		4,520		2,250		2,270
Export		1,000		480		250		230
Total Variable Cost @ Standard		10,000		5,000		2,500		2,500
Plant Variable Variance (Exhibit 2)						450		(450)
Inventory Adjustment (Exhibit 6)						(150)		150
Total Variable Cost @ Actual	10,000	10,000	5,000	5,000	2,500	2,800	2,500	2,200
Plant Fixed Cost (Exhibit 3)							(1,250)	(1,200)
Headquarters Fixed Cost (Exhibit 1)							(280)	(250)
Total Operating Income							970	750

responsible for those deviations were expected to explain the reason(s) for the variances.

Petrochem has had over 20 years experience with the standard direct costing system. The company felt that the system focuses needed management attention to costs related to volume. Two problems were noted. The first was the need to revise the chart of accounts so that variable and fixed costs are recorded separately. The second was that a number of people (at the corporate level in Petrochem) do not understand direct costing; and, of course, direct cost must be adjusted to full cost for financial accounting purposes.

Case Study Two

The second case study revolves around a small greeting card manufacturer, Caralot Cards. Caralot makes high quality greeting cards priced for the luxury end of the market, to be sold in department and specialty stores. Each of the six varieties of cards consists of a die cut paper card with a scented stuffed fabric "pillow" and various trimmings (for example, bows, lace, and ribbon).

The accountant, an outside CPA, performs both financial accounting and management advisory services. The firm's most pressing initial task was to stem the continuing losses. The accountant decided that breakeven analysis would give the owner a starting point in determining the sales/production volume necessary to realize a profit.

The first step was to classify all costs of the business as fixed or variable. This was done by applying managerial judgment to historical cost data. Ideally, variable costs would have been estimated by type of card because each type used different trims, and so on. However, insufficient data made that degree of detail impossible. Instead, an average variable cost was computed across all card varieties. Exhibit 8 lists the types of variable costs.

Exhibit 8
VARIABLE COSTS FOR CARALOT CARDS

Raw Materials:	Operating Supplies:
Die cut cards	Scent
Fabric	Glue
Bows	Polyfill
Ribbon/Lace	Thread
	Cellophane (for packaging)
Direct Labor	Depreciation on sewing machine

Marketing expense - commissions

To figure the average variable cost per card, total variable costs were calculated and divided by the number of cards produced. Initially, variable cost per card was $.98.

The accountant suggested several cost-cutting moves to reduce the variable costs. By going directly to the suppliers and buying in bulk, the manufacturer was able to reduce raw materials costs substantially. Direct labor also was reduced. Initially, the company produced in a cottage industry setting. Women working at home made the cards and were paid on a piece rate basis. Later that mode was abandoned and operations were centralized in one location. This enabled the owner to set up an assembly line, greatly reducing labor time per card, and thus direct labor cost. These cost reduction moves brought variable production cost per card down from $.98, to $.868, to $.68.

A comparative breakeven analysis was performed to show the relationship of costs to volume to profit. Exhibit 9 shows the breakeven point in units for three scenarios. Variable marketing and manufacturing costs were subtracted from sales price to get contribution margin. Contribution margin was then divided into quarterly fixed costs to find the number of cards which must be sold, per quarter and per month, just to cover costs.

Exhibit 9
BREAKEVEN ANALYSIS FOR CARALOT CARDS
MARCH 1, 1984

Sales Price	$1.50
Variable Manufacturing Cost	(.508)
Commission	(.225)
Contribution Margin	.407

Scenario One — Cover all fixed and variable costs.
($10,248.63)/.407 = 25,181 cards/quarter
8,394 cards/month

Scenario Two — Cover all fixed and variable costs, plus withdrawals of $1,800/month for the owner.
($10,248.63 + 5,400)/.407 = 38,449 cards/quarter
12,816 cards/month

Scenario Three — Cover all fixed and variable costs, plus withdrawals of $1,800/month for the owner, plus $500/month note repayment.
($10,248.63 + 5,400 + 1,500)/.407 = 42,134 cards/quarter
14,045 cards/month

The analysis shown in Exhibit 9 had a large impact on the owner. For the first time, a clear relationship between volume and profit had been demonstrated. Importantly, the analysis brought the accounting down to earth for the owner. She could easily grasp the importance of increasing card sales, relating the number of cards sold to total contribution margin and to her desire to earn an income and service her debt.

Once variable costs were under control, further spreadsheet analysis focused on fixed costs. Exhibit 10 shows a direct costing income statement for Caralot. Note that commissions are shown as a fixed expense. This is due to the unstable nature of the commissions. By the end of 1984, the accountant saw that commissions and volume sold did not maintain a steady relationship of $.225 per card. Therefore, she elected not to include a cost which fluctuated so much with variable costs.

Exhibit 10
PROFIT AND LOSS STATEMENT FOR CARALOT CARDS
FOR THE PERIOD ENDING DECEMBER 31, 1984

Sales (including freight out)		88,369.07	100.0
Variable Cost of Goods Sold		40,129.03	45.4
Contribution Margin		48,240.04	54.6
Fixed Expenses:			
Payroll - Administrative	6,817.36		7.7
Payroll Taxes	1,182.63		1.3
Expense Advance	100.00		.1
Interest Expense	6,276.86		7.1
Telephone	2,254.94		2.6
Commissions	8,571.71		9.7
Fees	744.12		.8
Freight & Postage - Out	3,056.45		3.5
Samples	788.09		.9
Display Boxes	3,460.35		3.9
Travel & Entertainment	1,411.55		1.6
Vehicle - Repairs & Maintenance	140.09		.2
Vehicle - Gas & Parking	900.65		1.0
Vehicle - Tags & Licenses	156.75		.2
Vehicle - Insurance	222.80		.3
Accounting & Legal	3,340.65		3.8
Advertising	5,246.05		5.9
Rent	5,370.00		6.1
Insurance	355.39		.4
Office Supplies	3,572.89		4.0
Service Charges	300.03		.3
Janitorial	548.17		.6
Dues & Subscriptions	56.23		.1
Repairs & Maintenance	166.20		.2
Depreciation - Off Furniture	274.55		.3
Depreciation - Off Fixtures	827.01		.9
Depreciation - Vehicles	333.82		.4
Miscellaneous	1,380.94		1.6
Total Fixed Expense		57,856.28	65.5
Profit (Loss)		(9,616.24)	10.8

Exhibit 10 shows a loss for the year. Note that while monthly draws of $1,800 were not included as a fixed expense, they were occurring. The owner was living on borrowed money. Alternatives were either to cut costs still more or to increase volume.

Some fixed costs had been reduced by year's end. For example, display boxes expense (in which cards were displayed in department stores) was reduced from over $8,000 to $3,460.35 by buying directly from the supplier. Similarly, advertising expense was reduced by cutting out the middleman. Other fixed expenses did not seem amenable to cost cutting; therefore, the only way to earn a profit was to increase volume. By the end of 1984, this company was aggressively seeking out new markets and was selling cards in nearly all 50 states.

The breakeven analysis performed for this firm had a strong motivational impact on the owner. She was able to understand the analysis and translate it into a production and sales plan. In particular, it focused attention on the steps necessary to turn a loss into a profit.

Case Study Three

The third case study concerns efforts by MedCenter, a comprehensive care regional hospital, to update its cost accounting system to provide more relevant data for management decision making. The hospital is expanding its database so that costs can be organized by cost center (such as radiology, laboratory), admitting physician, and product (such as hernia repair, lens implant). These data then are used for cost control and planning purposes.

MedCenter uses fixed and variable cost breakdowns for budgeting. Prior to 1984, MedCenter accumulated total costs by cost center and projected future costs from them. Exhibit 11 shows 1983 costs broken out by cost center. Using their old procedures, the 1984 budget would have been compiled by multiplying expected 1984 service units (for example, patient days, surgeries) by 1983 total cost per unit. An error in budgeting was not serious as third-party reimbursement of all costs was the norm. However, MedCenter is facing a radically new reimbursement system. Medicare, which covers approximately 40% of MedCenter's patients, now reimburses the hospital according to diagnosis related groups (DRGs) — the 467 disease classifications under the prospective payment system. In other words, Medicare pays a set fee based on product rather than based on the cost of the inputs used (such as sutures, drugs, days a room is occupied). When reimbursement was based on costs, there was little incentive for cost control, and a nonprofit hospital could maintain zero profit relatively easily. Prospective payment raises the very real prospect of operating losses. Hence, investigation of costs versus revenues takes on increased importance.

In preparing the 1984 budget, MedCenter used both managerial judgment and the high-low method to separate fixed and variable costs. The high-low method was applied to determine fixed and variable cost components because monthly data were believed to be unreliable and, therefore, insufficient data existed for analysis by regression. Preliminary analysis of the data led MedCenter's controller to conclude that simply applying the high-low method to the

Exhibit 11
COSTS FOR 1983

Cost Center:	Unit Description	Number	Total Cost	Cost
Routine Services:				
Adult and Pediatric	Patient days	30,137	4,417,693	$ 146.59
ICU	Patient days	858	493,808	575.53
Newborn	Patient days	2,722	322,041	118.31
Operating Room and Sterile Supply	Surgeries	3,291	788,591	239.62
Recovery Room	Occasions	2,357	46,687	19.81
Delivery Room	Deliveries	1,035	436,366	421.61
Anesthesiology	Surgeries	3,291	29,014	8.82
Radiology	Exams	19,719	986,580	50.03
Laboratory	Tests	297,934	1,096,615	3.68
Nuclear Medicine	Scans	898	119,142	132.67
Electrocardiology	Examinations	3,402	72,257	21.24
Physical Therapy	Treatments	11,551	224,358	19.42
Electroencephalogram	Examinations	236	38,680	163.90
Respiratory Therapy	Hours	50,254	218,325	4.34
Ultra Sound	Treatments	1,059	86,722	81.89
Blood Bank	Transfusions	888	101,501	114.30
Occupational Therapy	Days	2,497	36,861	15.56
Emergency Room	Occasions	13,349	970,467	72.70
Medical and Surgical Supplies	Markup			
Pharmacy	Markup			
Intravenous Solutions	Markup			

1982 and 1983 data would be inappropriate. Specifically, all cost centers had experienced increased costs (for example, wage increases) and most had purchased additional capital equipment. For example, radiology had added CAT scan capability in 1983. Therefore, he decided to adjust the 1982 data to reflect the 1983 changes.

Exhibit 12
ADJUSTED COSTS FOR 1983 AND 1982

Cost Center	Unit Description	1983		1982	
		Units	Total Cost	Units	Total Cost
Routine Services:					
Adult	Patient days	30,137	$4,417,783	33,485	$4,493,017
Newborn	Patient days	2,722	322,040	3,106	326,671
Operating Room	Surgeries	3,291	788,589	3,400	794,936
Radiology	Exams	19,719	986,542	20,261	1,006,157

Exhibit 12 shows 1983 data for several cost centers as well as 1982 data adjusted to reflect 1983 prices and capital purchases. The high-low method was applied to these adjusted data to determine fixed and variable cost components. For example, the $75,234 difference in cost for routine services—adult divided by the 3,348 change in patient days yielded a variable rate of $22.47 per patient day. Fixed costs for routine services—adult were $3,740,609. The variable component is composed of linens and laundry, services of aides and orderlies, housekeeping, and some utilities and supplies. The large fixed component reflects professional nursing services, some utilities, and furniture, fixtures, and medical equipment. Exhibit 13 gives the variable rates and fixed cost components for the cost centers listed in Exhibit 12.

Exhibit 13
VARIABLE AND FIXED COMPONENTS OF COST

Cost Center	Variable Rate	Fixed Cost
Routine Services:		
Adult	$22.47/day	$3,740,609
Newborn	12.06/day	289,213
Operating Room	58.23/surgery	596,954
Radiology	36.19/exam	272,911

The use of fixed and variable costs made preparation of the 1984 budget simpler and prepared the way for the use of flexible budgeting to determine cost variances. Previously, actual costs based on actual level of activity were compared with budgeted costs based on totally different levels of activity. MedCenter expects to see improved cost forecasting and more valuable performance evaluation as a result of fixed and variable cost identification.

Chapter 7

Summary and Conclusions

An analysis of fixed and variable costs can be very important to a company. Its usefulness cuts across industry and size boundaries. "The ability to track variable costs accurately is the key to profitability," remarked one survey respondent. Another noted that fixed and variable expense analysis helped provide an advantage over the competition — a "financial edge."

The trend in the use of fixed and variable expense analysis is upward. This is to be expected because management accounting as a field is gaining increased recognition. Naturally, the tools of the management accountant are becoming more widely understood and used.

The increased recognition of the value of fixed and variable expense analysis is clear in reading the professional literature. Article after article describes decision-making techniques which rely on the input of fixed and variable cost data. Chapter 4 discusses accounting articles which are concerned with fixed and variable costing. Very few deal with cost separation methods; perhaps accounting authors believe textbooks do an adequate job of explaining them. Instead, most of the literature focuses on applications of fixed and variable costs to decision making. Fixed and variable expense analysis is advocated for a wide variety of applications, including: planning, pricing, profitability analysis, capital asset purchases, and breakeven analysis. The annotated bibliography at the end of this book lists a number of articles and books in addition to those reviewed in previous sections. Interested readers can locate additional references to fixed and variable cost separation and use in the annotated bibliography.

In order to obtain more current information, a survey of 25 companies which use fixed and variable expense analysis was conducted.

The telephone and personal interviews, which comprised the survey, elicited information on the benefits and problems of separating and using these costs. Successful firms involved in using fixed and variable cost analysis do so with a healthy degree of caution. They use textbooks and the literature as guidelines, modifying the techniques, as it becomes necessary, to suit their particular circumstances. Managerial judgment was cited, most frequently, as the way these firms separate fixed from variable costs.

The use of statistical methods for cost separation probably will increase in the future, primarily because of the increasing availability of personal computers and related software. The spreadsheet analysis presented in Case Study Two will become more common — as management accountants ask "what if" questions for planning. Even so, the inputs and outputs of the computer process will continue to be tempered with managerial judgment. This may be one reason why managerial judgment is used so widely to separate fixed and variable costs. Judgment is necessary when using the costs and performing the analysis, so it is natural to extend the method back to cost separation. As Case Study Three demonstrated, managerial judgment is compatible with computational separation methods. Clearly, many management accountants believe managerial judgment provides good results. Some voiced concerns over their inability to deal with semivariable costs, but most echoed the CPA who, when asked if he had encountered any problems in separating fixed and variable costs, replied, "none that I can't ignore." As long as errors in classifying semivariable costs are immaterial, managerial judgment will remain the cost separation method of choice.

In reviewing the survey results, it became apparent that fixed and variable cost use is a valuable decision-making aid. However, there is no one simple way to separate fixed from variable costs, or one way to use them. Instead, the theme that runs through the accounting literature and results of the survey is diversity. This diversity is grounded in the individual's thorough knowledge of the company's cost structure, a knowledge gained from accounting courses, reading professional journals, talking with colleagues and consultants, and observing what is going on in the company, the industry, and the rest of the world.

The different ways in which fixed and variable expense analysis can be used are illustrated further in the case studies. Case Study One describes the direct standard costing system of a large petroleum refinery. All costs of production are classified either as fixed or as variable. Income statements are cast in a direct costing framework.

This company has found direct costing to be of primary value in budgeting and of secondary value in cost control.

Case Study Two presents the way a small greeting card manufacturer uses fixed and variable costs to construct breakeven points under a number of different assumptions. The classification of costs as fixed and variable has clarified the profit-volume relationship for the owner and has led to increased emphasis on cost control and marketing (that is, increasing sales volume).

Case Study Three shows how a hospital combines the high-low method and managerial judgment to separate fixed and variable costs. The separation of costs according to behavior has led to increased confidence in the budgeting process.

In summary, this book has sought to examine fixed and variable expense analysis from various perspectives. The goal is to provide the management accountant with sufficient material to tailor a program to suit his or her specific needs.

Appendix

Survey for Fundamentals of Cost Behavior: Separating and Using Costs as Fixed and Variable

Company _____

Type Firm: ____ Manufacturing
             ____ Service
             ____ Nonprofit
             ____ SIC Code

Name of Interviewee _____

Title of Interviewee _____

Address _____

         _____

         _____

Phone Number ( ) _____

Net Sales Revenue for most recently completed
     fiscal year _____

    This survey is part of a National Association of Accountants study on separating and using costs as fixed and variable. We need your help in determining whether or not firms actually separate costs into these two components and, if so, how these costs are used.

    The definition of variable cost is: a cost which changes in total in proportion to changes in the volume of the main activities of an enterprise (for example, a firm or division). Thus, a variable cost is reasonably constant on a per unit of volume basis over a defined range of activity (sometimes called the "relevant range") and for a given time frame.

The definition of a fixed cost is: a cost which is constant in total within a given, though perhaps wide, but defined range of activity (sometimes called the "relevant range") and for a given time frame.

1.   Does your company's management use fixed and variable cost classifications for any of the following purposes? (If no, go to question 11.)

     _____ planning
     _____ reporting
     _____ decision-making
     _____ evaluation
     _____ other

2.   Do fixed and variable expense classifications appear on regular reports to management? If so, what kind of reports?

3.   For what specific purpose(s) does your firm use fixed/variable costs?

     _____ budgeting
     _____ capital expenditures
     _____ special orders
     _____ variance analysis
     _____ direct costing
     _____ breakeven analysis
     _____ pricing
     _____ profitability analysis, existing products
     _____ profitability analysis, new products
     _____ other (list)

4.   Who decides how costs are to be divided into fixed and variable components?

5. What methods are used to divide costs into fixed and variable components?

_____ managerial judgment
_____ engineering and/or work management
_____ statistical methods
        _____ high-low
        _____ scatterplot
        _____ OLS
        _____ other (explain)

6. Some firms categorize account titles as strictly fixed or strictly variable. If your firm uses this method,

a. How long ago was this done?

b. Are these classifications updated?

7. Does your firm recognize any costs as semivariable or mixed?

8. What are some bases used to describe variable costs at your firm? For example, variable utilities expense can be expressed as $ per unit produced, or $ per machine hour.

9. Costs generally are considered to be fixed or variable within some boundaries — the relevant range.

a. How sensitive to volume changes are your fixed and variable costs?

b. What is the relevant range for your firm?

10. In theory, all costs are variable over the long run; costs are fixed only for the short run.

    a. How long is the period for which you typically consider costs as fixed?

    b. Does this time period change depending on the type of cost or type of decision?

11. Is fixed and variable cost information used informally; for example, is management aware of it even though it may not be a part of the formal reporting process? (For instance, management may have knowledge of the fixed/variable components of various expenses and may use that knowledge in decision making even though the expenses are never broken down that way on paper.)

12. Would you like to see more use of fixed/variable costing in your firm? If yes, for what purposes?

13. Do you think that the appropriateness of fixed and variable cost breakdowns depends on particular factors such as:

    _____ firm size
    _____ number of products
    _____ type of product
    _____ type of department/division
    _____ other

14. Do you think information on fixed and variable costs would be of use to external parties? Does your firm provide such information?

15. Have you encountered any problems in separating and/or using fixed and variable costs?

16. We certainly appreciate your help in responding to this questionnaire. Would you mind if your name and company affiliation were published in this study in a list of contributors?

    _____ yes, by name and company
    _____ yes, company listing only
    _____ no

Annotated Bibliography

A number of articles and books deal with the subject of cost behavior to a greater or lesser extent. Some of these are listed below with a brief description of their relevance to separating and using fixed and variable costs. The following legend identifies the primary emphasis of the source:

A — application, shows a use for fixed/variable costs but assumes reader can handle cost separation.

C — characteristics of fixed/variable costs are discussed.

M — methods for separating fixed and variable costs.

A   Abel, Rein, "The Role of Costs and Cost Accounting in Price Determination," *Management Accounting*, April 1978, pp. 29-32.
         In imperfectly competitive markets, segregation of fixed and variable costs is important when preparing data for pricing purposes.

A   Amante, Joseph R., and Robert L. Graham, "Flexible Budgeting — A Defense Industry Approach," *Management Accounting*, February 1974, pp. 37-38.
         Flexible budgeting can be an important tool. Fixed costs should be omitted in the short run because the manager has no control over them. The manager's attention can be directed toward variable expenses.

C   Atack, W. A. J., and Glyden O. Headley, "Have Accountants Failed Government?" *Cost and Management*, January/February 1984, pp. 4-12.
         Corporate accountants have a limited understanding of cost behavior, yet knowledge of cost behavior is vital to managerial decision making. Performance measurement and cost-benefit studies have been carried out, but too little attention has been given to proper classification and measurement of costs.

A   Barret, Timothy F., "Variance Analysis of Variable Overhead," *Management Accounting* (Brit.), June 1978, pp. 252-254.
         The use of multiple absorption rates, one for each base of cost

variability, will give an exact analysis of the total variable-overhead variance. Using one absorption rate, the choice of the base may lead to sub-analysis of the total variable-overhead variance. Separate standard costs will allow more detailed analysis.

A   Bleil, Gordon B., "Understanding Financial Analysis Techniques — The 11th Hour for Marketers," *Bank Marketing*, December 1982, pp. 11-15.

Application of cost accounting concepts, including fixed and variable costs, to bank marketing.

A   Blum, James D., and Leroy D. Brooks, "Income Distortion in Accounting for Fixed Costs," *Review of Business and Economic Research*, Winter 1976-77, pp. 69-78.

Income distortion has existed with absorption costing which may be inherent either in the method or in management manipulation. Direct costing is tentatively the most desirable costing method. The possibility of manipulation is limited. Direct costing and relevant costing will give the same stated income.

C   Bruegelman, Thomas M., Gaile A. Haessly, Michael Schiff, and Claire P. Wolfangel, *The Use of Variable Costing in Pricing Decisions*, National Association of Accountants, 1985.

This report details the results of a survey of company executives responsible for pricing. Variable costs are used as a basis for setting prices in strategic, or short-run, situations. Full costs were generally used in routine pricing decisions.

C   Burritt, Roger L., and Peter F. Luckett, "Direct Costing — Is It Allocation Free?" *Management International Review*, Fourth Quarter 1982, pp. 34-44.

The variable-fixed cost division dominates direct costing proposals, but when allocation dimension is included, that division must be made explicit. Direct costing, based on variability of costs, doesn't avoid cost allocation but avoids allocation of fixed manufacturing costs.

A   Chastain, Clark E., "How Management Accountants Coped with the Recession," *Management Accounting*, January 1985, pp. 34-38.

Companies successfully riding out the recession engaged in a number of cost-cutting measures. In particular, fixed costs were trimmed by restructuring the company to drop less profitable operations and increase volume in the remaining plants. The importance of maintaining adequate cash flow was examined.

A   Cherry, Donald C., and Charles J. Dirksen, "Analyzing Changes in Cost: A General Computerized Approach," *Cost and Management*, May/June 1983, pp. 26-33.

Variance analysis is used to determine why costs change from one period to another, or why they are greater or less compared to some standard or budget. Both variable and total cost variances are calculated.

A   Cosh, Andrew M., "Computerized Cost Classification System," *Management Accounting,* April 1972, pp. 42-45.

The variable cost classification system is suggested for use in storing cost elements. Data can be retrieved when management needs an answer to specific and immediate problems.

C   Davies, J. E., "An Analysis of Cost and Supply Conditions in the Liner Shipping Industry," *Journal of Industrial Economics,* June 1983, pp. 417-435.

The behavior of short-run and long-run costs is examined with respect to the liner shipping industry. High fixed costs have led companies to cooperate in planning and capacity utilization.

A   Davies, J. R., "Determining the 'Plus' in Cost-Plus Pricing," *Management Accounting* (Brit.), May 1978, pp. 198-200.

A base price must be determined such that below this price a firm suffers a loss. This base is equal to variable cost. Fixed and variable costs may not fall clearly into one category.

A   Eichhorn, Frederic G., "A Direct Allocation Financial Data Base for Manufacturing," *Management Accounting,* May 1978, pp. 39-42, 46.

The financial reporting data base gives management the ability to generate direct, allocation, or a combination of the direct and allocation reports at the end of the period.

C,M   Elliot, Larry W., "Cost Behavior — A Dynamic Concept," *Management Accounting,* March 1974, pp. 33-36, 41.

Cost behavior is seen to depend on the expectation period (that is, short run or long run).

A   Finkler, Steven A., "Cost Finding for High-Technology, High-Cost Services: Current Practice and a Possible Alternative," *Health Care Management Review,* Summer 1980, pp. 17-29.

Determination of fixed and variable cost components is a first step in creating a vertical cost-finding system for hospitals. Vertical cost-finding is oriented toward the cost of final products/programs (for example, open-heart surgery).

C,M   Garrison, Ray H., *Managerial Accounting,* (3rd ed.) Business Publications, Inc., Plano, Texas, 1982.

Chapters 2 and 5 present an introduction to cost-behavior analysis.

C   Ghosh, B. C., "New Definition of Fixed Costs in Break-Even Analysis," *Management Accounting,* May 1980, pp. 50-51.

Reconciles traditional break even analysis with absorption costing by adjusting fixed overhead.

A,C   Govindarajan, V., and Robert N. Anthony, "How Firms Use Cost Data in Price Decisions," *Management Accounting*, July 1983, pp. 30-36.

A survey of industrial companies shows that most companies use full cost in pricing products. Results showed relatively few firms use variable costing.

C   Gross, Stephen, and Paul F. Dienemann, "A Model for Estimating Aerospace Industry Contractor Overhead Costs," *Engineering and Process Economics*, January 1978, pp. 61-74.

The degree of variability for overhead cost categories of aerospace defense contractors was investigated using ordinary least squares. Costs were found to be semivariable in each case.

A   Hartman, Bart P., "The Management Accountant's Role in Deleting a Product Line," *Management Accounting*, August 1983, pp. 63-66.

The problems faced by a floor covering distributor in determining whether or not to drop outdoor carpet lines are detailed. Author notes that "the principles of cost-volume-profit relationships were applied in decision making. Management became aware of the presence and importance of fixed and variable costs.

C,M   Horngren, Charles T., *Introduction to Management Accounting*, (6th ed.) Prentice-Hall, Englewood Cliffs, N.J., 1984.

Chapters 2 and 8 define fixed and variable costs and describe methods of analyzing cost behavior.

A   Johnson, A. P., "Multiple-Service Costing," *Journal of the Operational Research Society*, June 1978, pp. 551-558.

Multiple-service costing allocates fixed costs of services to the demands, based on consideration of the interacting system of supply and demand.

A   Johnson, Douglas A., Steven Kaplan, and Bill B. Hook, "Looking for Mr. Overhead: An Expanded Role for Management Accountants," *Management Accounting*, November 1983, pp. 65-68.

This article discusses the role of the accountant in the management team. It notes the importance of a knowledge of cost behavior. Specific examples of ways used by Motorola, Inc. to enhance accounting reports are shown.

A   Keegan, Daniel P., "A New Tool That Minimizes Pricing Guesswork," *Price Waterhouse Review*, 1984, pp. 22-32.

C   Laszlo, Peter J., "How Variable are Direct Wages?" *Management Accounting* (Brit.), October 1978, pp. 386-387.

Traditionally, labor is thought to be a strictly variable cost. In actual practice, factors do not allow for absolute control over labor costs. A survey shows the degree of fixity of labor costs and firms' methods of accounting for them.

C   Lere, John C., "Observable Differences Among Prime, Variable, and Absorption Costing Firms," *Journal of Business Research,* September 1980, pp. 371-387.
Firms may use absorption costing, variable costing, or prime costing. Cost structure best distinguishes firms choosing different methods. Variables focusing on the methods' impact on net income figures and the importance of various uses within the firm are less useful in predicting what cost method a firm uses.

C,A   Littrell, Earl K., "The High Tech Challenge to Management Accounting," *Management Accounting,* October 1984, pp. 33-36.
This article discusses the impact of the product life cycle on management accounting. The author notes that in the growth stage of production the relevant range keeps changing and the distinction between fixed and variable costs is blurred. ". . . fixed costs tend to fade into semi-fixed or even variable status."

C,M   Matz, Adolph, and Milton F. Usry. *Cost Accounting: Planning and Control,* (8th ed.) South-Western Publishing Co., Cincinnati, 1984.
Chapter 16 offers a comprehensive treatment of cost-behavior analysis.

M   May, Gordon S., and James P. Bedingfield, "An Additional Dimension to Cost Analysis: Freehand Regression," *RIA Cost and Management,* November/December 1977, pp. 38-41.
Freehand regression is used to separate fixed and variable costs. It is similar to the scatterplot method, yet includes confidence bands.

A   Mills, William B., "Drawing Up a Budgeting System for an Ad Agency," *Management Accounting,* December 1983 (65), pp. 46-51, 59.
A complete case study of the implementation of a cost accounting system in an ad agency is presented. The system relies on the separation of costs into fixed and variable components. The utility of the system for budgeting and profitability analysis is demonstrated.

C   Mintz, Gilbert, "Bottomline Approach for DP Managers," *Data Management,* August 1978, pp. 16-17.
Data processing equipment should be structured using small cost increments to approach the notion of variable costs as nearly as possible. Flexibility is very important and businesses should not commit to long-term leases as technical advances will steal benefits

away. Timesharing offers truly variable cost arrangements for data processing.

M   Mirman, Leonard J., Dov Samet, and Yair Tauman, "An Axiomatic Approach to the Allocation of a Fixed Cost Through Prices," *Bell Journal of Economics,* Spring 1983, pp. 139-151.

Short-run fixed costs are allocated through Aumann-Shapley prices, which allocate joint costs of production to each of the individual products. Long-run cost functions do not usually contain a fixed cost component. A part of the A-S prices associated with the long-run cost is allocated to fixed cost and part is allocated to the variable cost of the short-run costs.

M   Nagy, Joseph E., "Hospitals Must Identify Fixed and Variable Costs," *Hospital Financial Management,* March 1982, pp. 50-54.

Hospital managers should analyze costs by segregating all costs into fixed and variable categories. Each category consists of two costs: 1. committed and discretionary fixed costs, and 2. pure and step variable costs.

C   National Association of Accountants, "Management Uses of Fixed and Variable Expense Analysis," unpublished study by Management Accounting Practices staff, April 1, 1980.

The NAA investigated the applicability of management's analysis of fixed and variable expenses to financial reporting. A survey of manufacturing firms yielded the following results: Many large firms use fixed and variable expense reporting for internal purposes, and the most widely used cost separation method is managerial judgment.

C   Owens, Robert W., "Cash Flow Variance Analysis," *Accounting Review,* January 1980, pp. 111-116.

Variable cost quantity variance and price variance should be stated in dollars of incremental cash flow. To compare this cash flow approach with the more common textbook approach, it is necessary to divide variable costs into a non-storable category (direct and indirect labor) and a storable category (raw materials and supplies). This is done because costs are identical at the time of purchase and at the time of use only for non-storable variable cost items.

A   Pakkala, A. L., "Fixed Costs Impact Earnings Predictions," *Financial Analysts Journal,* January/February 1979, pp. 46-48.

Investment analysis and financial forecasting can be improved if the analysis includes both fixed and variable cost information, rather than more limited data on total costs alone.

M,A   Peterson, Virginia M., "Determining Cost of Services, Break-Even Analysis, and Pricing," *Fund Raising Management,* December 1983, pp. 54-57.

Total variable costs (primarily personnel) are calculated separately from fixed costs. Knowing the variable cost per service and the allocated fixed cost, various break-even volumes and prices can be determined.

A   Roche, Tony, "Adopt the Logical Approach to Questions of Standard Costing," *Accountancy,* August 1978, pp. 103-104.
Fixed and variable overhead can be separated by regression analysis. Fixed overhead is budgeting along with the expected production volume. Variable overhead is calculated to vary directly with production.

A   Saunders, Gary, "Evaluating the Effect of Stockouts and Reorder Points on the EOQ," *Cost and Management,* March/April 1982, pp. 38-41.
Larricks Corp. developed an iterative method which evaluates the effects of stockouts and reorder points on the EOQ through a comparison of total variable costs.

A   Schwartzbach, Henry R. and Richard G. Vangermeersch, "Why We Should Account for the 4th Cost of Manufacturing," *Management Accounting,* July 1983, pp. 24-28.
The impact of an increasingly mechanized workplace on cost accounting is discussed. The authors suggest that "machine labor" be accounted for in addition to materials, labor, and factory overhead. The importance of determining fixed and variable costs in developing a cost accounting system for the capital-intensive firm is stressed.

C,A   Seed, Allen H., III, "Cost Accounting in the Age of Robotics," *Management Accounting,* October 1984, pp. 39-43.
The author argues that costs should be classified according to behavior, and that conversion cost should replace the direct labor burden breakdown. The impact of automation on fixed and variable costs also is noted.

A   Sharav, Itzhak, "Cost Justification Under the Robinson-Patman Act," *Management Accounting,* July 1978, pp. 15-22.
Businesses base decisions on marginal cost principles, which would induce them to take larger orders at a discount price in order to utilize capacity and spread fixed costs. A suggested technique is to assign prices based on the costs, assuming complete utilization. Then, for situations of underutilization, prices should be increased to compensate for unabsorbed fixed costs.

C   Skinner, R. C., "Accounting Information for Decision Making," *In-*

ternational *Journal of Accounting Education,* Fall 1971, pp. 65-78.
Relates fixed and variable nature of costs to short, intermediate, and long runs.

C   Smith, Alan F., "Overhead Variance Analysis — It's as Simple as ABC," *Management Accounting,* October 1982, pp. 32-35.
Fixed and variable costs often are changed by the implementation of decisions, the influx of time, or by a new planning period. A flexible method of variance analysis allows overhead costs to be categorized according to the type and level of decision.

A   Smith, August, and Kenneth Smith, "The Effects of Variable Costing in Break-Even Analysis," *National Public Accountant,* July 1976, pp. 12-14.
Variable costs are affected by a number of factors such as the indirect labor of management, the direct labor used in making the product, and so on. Accurate determination of variable costs is important in breakeven analysis.

C,A   Taylor, Sam G., "Optimal Aggregate Production Strategies for Plants with Semifixed Operating Costs," *AIIE Transactions,* September 1980, pp. 253-257.
Semifixed costs can be saved when the plant is temporarily shut down. Optimization techniques may be used to develop optimal strategies for a single production line with semifixed operating and linear variable costs.

A   Turk, Frederick J., "A Tool for Planning and Decision Making," *Management Focus,* March/April 1980, pp. 8-13.
Breakeven analysis is discussed in relation to planning in higher education. The importance of cost separation for this purpose is emphasized.

C,A   Whiting, Edwin, "Fixed/Variable Cost: Beware!" *Accountancy,* May 1981, pp. 74, 77-78.
Problems associated with the use of fixed and variable costs are discussed. Costs are more fixed as volume of output declines but proportionately less fixed as it expands. Fixed costs from one cost center can be variable in another. Distinguishing between fixed/variable costs is important because it provides the data for cost-profit-volume analysis and controllable and noncontrollable costs.

A   Wolf, Warren G., "Developing a Cost System for Today's Decision Making," *Management Accounting,* December 1982, pp. 19-23.
This article describes a "Fully Integrated Direct Costing System." Determination of fixed and variable costs is crucial to the implemen-

tation of this sytstem. Other costs used are prime, direct and full absorption. Three variances, usage, efficiency and rate are calculated for materials, labor, and overhead.

A   Zelman, William N., Bruce P. Newman, James D. Suver, and Donald R. Simons, "Managing Rate Adjustments by Health Care Providers/Comment," *Health Services Research,* Summer 1983, pp. 165-181.
   Administrators must be able to evaluate the effect of cost and volume changes on the rate structure more than once a year to be able to make timely decisions.

National Association of Accountants
Committee on Research

1985-86

Donald W. Baker, CMA
Chairman
Southwire Co.
Carrollton, Ga.

Paul Aikman
Aikman and Co.
Hilton Head Island, S.C.

George Bannon
Moravian College
Bethlehem, Pa.

James W. Brackner
Utah State University
Logan, Utah

James P. Colford
IBM Corp.
Tarrytown, N.Y.

Arthur V. Corr, CMA
University of Wisconsin-Parkside
Kenosha, Wis.

James L. Crandall
Munroe Egg Farm, Inc.
Plainfield, Ill.

Dennis C. Daly, CMA
University of Minnesota
Minneapolis, Minn.

Gail W. DeLong
Develco
San Diego, Calif.

Mohamed S. Eisa
Southern University
Baton Rouge, La.

Robert Fox
Creative Output, Inc.
Milford, Conn.

Charles L. Grant
Becton Dickinson & Co.
Hunt Valley, Md.

Ronald W. Hall
Southwestern Bell Telecom
St. Louis, Mo.

Glendon R. Hildebrand
First National Bank of Chicago
Chicago, Ill.

Ronald L. Leach
Eaton Corp.
Cleveland, Ohio

Donald J. McCarty, Jr.
RCA Laboratories
Princeton, N.J.

Sherman R. Roser
St. Cloud State University
St. Cloud, Minn.

Arjan T. Sadhwani
University of Akron
Akron, Ohio

Gene L. Smith, CMA
BF Goodrich
Akron, Ohio

Mildred B. Stephens
Educational Testing Service
Princeton, N.J.

Robert B. Sweeney
Memphis State University
Memphis, Tenn.

Manuel A. Tipgos
University of Kentucky
Lexington, Ky.

David W. Vogel
E.I. du Pont de Nemours & Co.
Wilmington, Del.

Thomas H. Williams
University of Wisconsin
Madison, Wis.

Robert C. Young
Digital Equipment Corp.
Merrimack, N.H.